man turned in
on himself:
understanding sin
in 21ST- century america

heather choate davis

ICKTANK
PRESS

MAN TURNED IN ON HIMSELF:
UNDERSTANDING SIN IN 21st-CENTURY AMERICA.

Cover Design: Lon Davis

cover art

Erica L. Grimm
This Present Moment: Death and Dying Done
Encaustic, steel and 23K gold on birch panel

egrimmvance.com

about the artist

Erica is a Canadian artist, researcher, and educator whose work is exhibited widely and is in collections such as the Canada Council Art Bank and the Richmond Art Gallery. Invited Nash Lecturer and Distinguished Alumnae from the University of Regina, she is Associate Professor and Chair, Art + Design Department, School of the Arts, Media and Culture at Trinity Western University.

Erica's material practice is rooted in embodiment and she is curious about liminal, saturated or otherwise inexplicable but ordinary experiences. Her visual images layer minimal planes of material, texts, maps, medical imagery, drawn fragments, projected video and aural soundscapes, exploring how material surfaces (and sounds) unfold depth and collide to create meaning. Her written practice inquires into the epistemological implications of the process of making. Written from the vantage point of a maker of art, the *Aesthetics of Attentiveness*, opens with being "stopped" by a heart attack, ends with a laugh and identifies recurrent phases of aesthetic acts–the necessity of being stopped; trusting unknowing and self-emptying attentiveness through the act of making; emerging out of this liminal process with a laugh of insight having made something that surprises even the artist. The *Aesthetics of Attentiveness* is forthcoming from Wilfred Laurier University Press.

contents

'O look, look in the mirror,
O look in your distress:
Life remains a blessing
Although you cannot bless.
'O stand, stand at the window
As the tears scald and start;
You shall love your crooked neighbor
With your crooked heart.'

W.H. Auden,
from *As I Walked Out One Evening*

introduction

We begin with a simple premise: "sin" is dead. Not the state of sin, of course, or our ever-proliferating sinful acts, but the word itself, and the impact of the word, which, for the better part of human history has helped individuals and communities recognize when they were "missing the mark."[1] In contemporary American culture, "sin" has been filed away with leeches and bloodletting and the stuff of *DaVinci Code* dramas. "Sin" is a big, wagging finger, a word that pronounces judgment and blame; it means that you've been bad, and, more often than not, sexual in a wholly unproductive way. With the launch of oral contraceptives and the women's liberation movement in the 1960s "a new age of permissiveness[2] was ushered in, "an unorchestrated attempt to shake off an oppressive Christianity that had terrorized the faithful with its doctrine of an angry and vengeful God."[3] In no time at all the word "sin" began to vanish from the culture, as fewer deeds—not merely sexual acts but pleasure-seeking and self-aggrandizement of all stripes—were regarded as such. The state of Original Sin, upon which the doctrine of the salvation hinges, became an artifact of the judgment era. A congenital state of sin was replaced with a simpler, easier to marginalize definition: sin, not as a condition but an act— little vices easily trivialized, rationalized, and, for the first time in history, entirely personal, "a matter between oneself and God."[4]

Wanting the freedom to pursue their own sinfulness in peace, Americans became far less judgmental. The less we spoke or thought of sin, the easier it was to believe that it had been transcended.

Clearly, any day in the life of the American narrative will reveal that we have not transcended sin. Nor have we "outgrown" the very human need to confess and atone for our sinful ways. Only now these acts are being played out in reality TV and afternoon talk shows,[5] rewarding viewers with a sense of superiority, and the shameful soul in the hot seat with "fifteen minutes of fame" —a far cry from eternal life. So how do we make the teachings of salvation relevant to a contemporary, sin-oblivious culture? With no grasp of sin, what is it people are supposed to think they're being saved from? And how, in our pluralistic society, can we find language that is not divisive, but rather helps create a universal understanding of our common brokenness and the price we all pay for the denial of sin and its consequences?

Ironically, the seeds of our answer may be found in the medieval teachings of St. Augustine. Although he is the church father considered largely responsible for equating sin with sex, his mature vision of sin was much broader and more useful: sin as incurvature, as man curved down towards his base roots and away from his divine birthright. A thousand years later, Martin Luther would build on Augustine's foundation of incurvature with a fully developed concept of *homo incurvatus in se*—man turned in on himself—or, sin as man turned towards his own interests and desires and away from relationship to others.

That American culture is a monument to individualism is not news, but increasingly we can see the cracks: isolation, depression, apathy, anxiety, narcissism, addiction. We have traded in the town square for laptops behind which we disappear, hide, seeking to dwell unchallenged in worlds of our own design, ideology, ambitions, pleasures, secrets, shame, terror. We are masters of our own free will, but still we cry out in the dark each night, "who will rescue me from this body of death?" (Romans 7:24) Even when real human contact is available, we choose to turn away, seeking solace and pleasure and release from sources that require little or nothing from us. Augustine pointed out this irony of sin long ago: "the choice of the will…is genuinely free only when it is not subservient to faults and sins."[6]

No, sin is not dead, but the term "is essentially obsolete."[7] If the Church cannot find a way to make it relevant again, to lead those who suffer daily from sin to call it by its name and follow "its awful glory"[8] to the cross, to the peace that passes all human understanding, then Christianity becomes little more than another feel-good flavor, or worse, a self-righteous nag. Sin as scarlet letter will no longer do the trick, but sin as *homo incurvatus in se* just might.

a word to the reader

The first chapter of this book is for the purpose of establishing the theological roots of *man turned in on himself.* In other words, it gives the work "street cred" with academics and theologians. It's very readable as these things go (and all the footnotes have been turned into endnotes to make it even more user-friendly) but if you're unaccustomed to reading theology for pleasure you might be unfamiliar with some of the references and be tempted to put the book aside. Please don't. If the early pages start to get a little too "insider baseball" for you, just skip to Chapter 2, where the dots will start being connected to history and contemporary social issues you don't need any background in to understand. That said, let's begin at the beginning....

chapter 1

the origins of *homo incurvatus in se:*
man turned in on himself

Picture a body curved inward—in the fetal position, for example. The shape of the curve does two things: 1) it protects and defends the thing it is turned in on, guarding it and the right to have it to oneself, preferably in the secret shadow of the curve, and 2) its curved form creates a barrier between the heart's desire and the things it wants to keep at bay: judgment, change, help, love, God. Even if we take God out of the conversation (a useful exercise when speaking of sin to a modern secularist), the image maintains its potency: when man is turned in on his own desires, the world— despite man's best efforts to the contrary— becomes smaller and darker. Without the impetus or wherewithal to reverse his course, his condition gets progressively worse. Without access to any power greater than himself—and with the sudden realization that he is, in fact, only human—he becomes trapped in the "hamster wheel" of his own thoughts and enslaved by his own feelings and desires. This universal human experience exposes the hard truth of the lie of sin:

> Wherefore it is not without meaning said that all sin is a lie. For no sin is committed save by that desire or will by which we desire that it be well with us, and shrink from it being ill with us. That, therefore, is a lie which we do in order that it may be well with us, but which makes us more miserable than we were.[9]
> —St. Augustine, *The City of God*

augustine on incurvature

St. Augustine wrote copiously on the subject of sin, but the first evidence that he was beginning to identify the shape of sin with a curve was in his commentary on the first psalm. The interpretation of the movement is subtle.

> *Blessed is the man who has not gone away in the counsel of the ungodly, nor stood in the way of sinners, and hath not sat in the seat of pestilence (Psalm 1: 1-2)*[10].

First, Augustine tells us that we are to identify the "he" in the psalm as Jesus Christ,[11] who is set apart, in these early lines, by what he *does not* do. He *does not* "go away," (or turn away) from God "as the man of the earth did."[12] While others "stand" stubbornly in their sinful state, Jesus does not, "for the enticements of the world held Him not."[13] Nor does He sit "in the seat of pestilence." Here, Augustine expands on "pestilence," a medieval term for sin, again, as the opposite of what Jesus would do:

> He willed not an earthly kingdom, with pride, which is well taken for 'the seat of pestilence'; for that there is hardly any one who is free from the love of rule, and craves not human glory. For a 'pestilence' is a disease widely spread, and involving all or nearly all.[14]

Three key concepts are introduced here: 1) that pride is the cornerstone of sin and the impetus for man's inward turn, 2) that pride is as widespread and destructive as disease, and 3) that individual sin generates consequences that spread and affect many, if not all.[15] In his summary of these lines we begin to see Augustine's gift for reflecting on the body and its physical movements to reveal the patterns of sinfulness:

> The order too of the words must be considered: "went away, stood, sat." For he "went away," when he drew back from God. He "stood," when

he took pleasure in sin. He "sat," when, confirmed in his pride, he could not go back, unless set free by Him.[16]

Went away. Stood. Sat. If we were to picture a continuum of positions in Augustine's thinking, these would comprise the central three of five. The first would be standing upright, heart lifted, arms outstretched and facing God. The next would be turning away with one's back to God. The third would be standing firmly in that opposition, arms likely crossed, followed by settling in so completely that one takes a seat. And finally, as the body has moved physically lower and further away from God, the last submission to sin—Stage 5, if you will— is to merely slump over, curved down to the earth like an animal:

> God made you as something good under him, and he made something lower on the scale, under you as well. . . . Don't give up the higher good and bow yourself down to the lower good. Be upright, and so be praised, because *all the upright of heart shall be praised* (Psalm 64:10). How is it that you sin, after all, but by treating the things you have received for your use in a disordered way, or out of turn? Be a good user of lower things, and you will be an upright enjoyer of the higher good.[17]

There are several concepts contained in this passage that are worth noting: 1) that "lower things" are not in themselves sinful, and that one can and should be a "good user" of them; 2) that the evil comes, rather, from our disordered desire for lower things,[18] which is foundational to Augustine's teaching of the Doctrine of Original Sin; and 3) that standing upright with hearts lifted is the position God intended for mankind. "It is incongruous to have the face looking upwards and the heart downwards."[19] Man is in the unique position of standing "with his feet in the center of the universe, able to stretch upward toward God or to contract back upon himself and fold himself away from God."[20] These are man's only choices: "All love either ascends or descends,"[21] according to Augustine. "The form given to man at creation exhorts him: *Sursum cor!*"[22] Lift up your heart!

And yet we choose to turn away, and down, curved back to the temporal and the lowly.

All incurvature begins with a "turn," as Scripture so often describes our rejection of God. "They will turn to other gods and serve them, despising me and breaking my covenant" (Deuteronomy 31:20). "All we like sheep have gone astray; we have all turned to our own way" (Isaiah 53:6). "All have turned away, they have together become worthless; there is no one who does good, not even one" (Romans 3:12). The seminal "turning away" of the Christian faith occurred in the Garden with the first act of disobedience, which came to be known as "the Fall." "Falling" and "turning away" are, for Augustine,

related ideas.[23] They are not one and the same, but the
first "fall" led to every turning away that followed—a
reality echoed in St. Paul's seminal verse: "Therefore,
just as sin came into the world through one man, and
death came through sin, and so death spread to all
because all have sinned" (Romans 5:12).

For Augustine, the Garden is not only the setting
of that first evil turn but also for God's exposition of His
divine model for interrelatedness:

> God chose to make a single individual the starting
> point of all mankind. . . . His purpose in this was
> that the human race should not merely be united
> in a society by natural likeness, but should also be
> bound together by a kind of tie of kinship to form
> a harmonious unity, linked together by the "bond
> of Peace."[24]

This interrelatedness would seem to constitute a
horizontal vision of God's will for mankind, and yet
Augustine's vision of incurvature is clearly a vertical one.
How is a reader to reconcile these ideas? One suggestion
would be to consider that Augustine himself never
reconciled them: he gave the world a fully developed
vision of love and the "bond of Peace" in the *City of God.*
He also gave the Church, in his early images of *curvatus*,
the "resources for later relational understandings of sin
which speak of sinful humanity as *homo incurvatus in
se.*"[25] Still, the paradox remains:

If for Augustine, sin is pride, it is not merely pride, but the willful re-direction of attention and love from God to the human self apart from God which results in alienation from God and the fracturing of human society.[26]

Augustine understood full well that the individual sin of pride—of curving inward—impacted the whole of the human family. But ultimately, he never adjusted his model of the vertical incurvature to accommodate this larger truth.

Now, having examined the principles behind—and the limitations of—Augustine's vertical movement, we look more closely at "turning," not simply away, but *towards* someone or something in His stead. It is essential to note that it is not the *subject* of desire that is evil: "For when the will abandons what is above itself, and turns to what is lower, it becomes evil—not because that is evil to which it turns, but because the turning itself is wicked."[27] In a sermon he delivered between 400-420 AD, Augustine challenges congregants who seem to be asking why, "if sin delights me,"[28] do we call it bad, and why, if it is bad did God create it in the first place? The examples he gives reveal that, for all our 21st-century advancements, our lusty wills haven't progressed at all. "If it is a sin to drink a lot, then why did God institute wine," Augustine asks from the pulpit, echoing the concerns of his flock. "If it's a sin to love gold . . . why did he create what it is wrong to love?"[29] Augustine flips the question on its head, reminding people that all that God created is good, and that these created things—wine, gold, savory meats—would be right to ask (if they were able) why, if the source of the world's troubles is the fact that man cannot use and enjoy created things in a manner that reflects love and good order, did God create man?[30] In potent and poetic form, Augustine makes it clear where the finger must point:

> For avarice is not a fault inherent in gold, but in the man who inordinately loves gold, to the detriment of justice, which ought to be held in incomparably higher regard than gold. Neither is luxury the fault of lovely and charming objects, but of the heart that inordinately loves sensual pleasures, to the neglect of temperance, which attaches us to objects more lovely in their spirituality, and more delectable by their incorruptibility. Nor yet is boasting the fault of human praise, but of the soul that is inordinately fond of the applause of men, and that makes light of the voice of conscience. Pride, too, is not the fault of him who delegates power, nor of power itself, but of the soul that is inordinately enamoured of its own power, and despises the more just dominion of a higher authority.[31]

He concludes with "pride" because, for Augustine, "pride is the beginning of sin."[32] The movement from pride to enslavement-to-sin can be seen in a continuum similar to that from standing upright to curving downward. The process begins when man catches a glimpse of the will of God. Understanding that what may be asked of him is to say *yes* to that which he'd rather refuse, and *no* to that which he longs to revel in, he responds by turning away to blaze his own trail. This turning is "itself a kind of conversion,"[33] where man becomes his own God, believing in his own will, reason, power, and choice above all else. Without the tempering effects of the Law or trust in God, he becomes unmoored, gravitating more and more towards his desires, which pull him farther away from the needs and desires of others, as well as from the life God had prepared especially for him. To justify this increasing defiance, "we first paint a distorted picture of our relation to God by pretending the relationship does not exist. At the same time . . . we enter into conflict in the human relationships which also make us who we are."[34] Having chosen to "remake" ourselves into sovereigns, with our own power and pleasure-seeking creeds, "we seek to entice or force others to also . . . move out of God's orbit and into ours."[35] And before long, we've reached that tipping point:

> Again, we see the irony of sin. God's justice hands man over to himself, just as man wanted. But the result is unexpected. The point was for man to be his own king, to have everything to himself under his own control; but he finds that his grasp for autonomy has led to slavery. He is at odds with himself, having become a nuisance to

himself, and is infinitely farther from the freedom he had desired.[36]

This well-tread path from pride to incurvature begins with the desire to be like God. This desire is not, in itself, a wrong impulse, as long as it is in the spirit of Scripture, e.g.: "Thus he has given us, through these things, his precious and very great promises, so that through them you may escape from the corruption that is in the world because of lust, and may become participants of the divine nature"(2 Peter 1:4). Rather, the sin is man's desire to make an end-run around God to achieve divine status on his own terms. "Since we are *not* gods *in se*, we can only become gods by participation in the true God."[37] This participation, according to Augustine's early reflections on the first psalm, is made possible by being "set free by Him, who neither 'hath gone away in the counsel of the ungodly, nor stood in the way of sinners, nor sat in the seat of pestilence.'"[38]

With that, the world takes a thousand-year pause on the subject of sin as incurvature. Although it is impossible to know the heart, mind, and written work of every Christian pastor and theologian from the 5th to the 16th century, Augustine's *curvatus* imagery does not appear to have been developed further until incurvature becomes *homo incurvatus in se* in the work of Martin Luther.

luther on *homo incurvatus in se*

The year was 1515. Martin Luther, a young professor of Biblical theology at the University of Wittenberg, was beginning his second series of lectures. The first had been on the Psalms; now he was turning his attention to the book of Romans. The progression of thought was so profound that Gordon Rupp noted "you could almost hear him growing in the night, so plain is the growth in maturity, independence and coherence in a few months."[39] To be specific, the greatest development was in "a more radical diagnosis of the sin of man, the seat of which, under all disguises and idolatries, is his egoism, lifting itself in rebellion against God."[40] For Luther, the tearing down of pride is the whole purpose of Romans;[41] it is at the heart of salvation because "the Spirit of God can arise only when the pride of the flesh has been humbled."[42] And so, on this point, Augustine and Luther are very much in agreement: pride is ground zero for sin and the impetus for man's choice to turn away from God, becoming *curvatus*. But there are several key differences in the two theologians' thinking about incurvature. The minor differences seem to extend logically from the primary ones, hitting many of the key doctrinal splits between Catholicism and the early Reformation along the way.

As we learned earlier, Augustine's view of incurvature reflects a vertical relationship between man and God in which man can—and must—choose between "directing his love up to the eternal or down to the temporal."[43] Not so with Luther, who sees the vertical paradigm as not only false but dangerous, leading him to build on the narrow definition of *curvatus* into a fully developed, cruciform view of *homo incurvatus in se*:

> For Augustine, sin consists in the fact that man is bent down to earth (*curvatus*) . . . but this means for Luther something quite different: it means that man is egocentric, that his will is determined by his own interest and so is bent upon itself (*incurvatus in se*). In Augustine, the sinful soul is "bent down" to earth; in Luther, it is "bent upon itself."[44]

The point of divide was likely born of Luther's "existential wranglings"[45] about how man could ever be good enough, or worthy enough, to merit God's grace. This period of torment led him to believe that he could not—that *we* could not—ever earn His love, but only through grace receive it, and catapulted a moment of divine insight into a theological revolution. Before Luther could begin to "reform" the curve from the vertical to the horizontal, he needed to dissect the flaws in Augustine's spectrum of movement from heaven to earth. This sends us back to the creedal turf of Pelagianism and man's role in his own salvation. Although defeated at the Council of Carthage (ironically, by the writings of Augustine), Pelagian precepts lived on in word and practice. Yes, it was agreed that the moment of conversion could only be attributed to God—that He did all, and we did nothing—but the indoctrination of works righteousness, of trying to live a life that was good enough to ensure salvation, continued to be central to the Christian faith up through the Reformation.

Now, consider the paradigm of Augustine's heavenly vs. earthly postures. We are either standing upright towards God, or curving down towards earth; the choice is entirely up to us. Luther's need to shift the notion of incurvature from the vertical to the horizontal no doubt stemmed from his observation that Augustine's model put man in the driver's seat, as if he could, if he tried hard enough, choose not to curve downwards. Luther's burgeoning doctrine of justification by faith alone cried out that this could never be so, that "'we of ourselves are by nature evil' and our evil inclination means that we cannot do good apart from grace."[46] The Church, according to Luther, is wrong to teach that works precede righteousness, that—even standing on tiptoes, arms outstretched to the point where they burst from the sockets—we could ever be upright enough. The key gift of this insight, of course, is that man may find not only salvation but also peace in acceptance of his own inescapable weakness. Better still, we are freed to accept our sinful, curved-in natures because we realize through grace that

'God loves sinners.' God saves no one but sinners,
He instructs no one but the foolish and stupid, He

enriches none but paupers, and He makes alive only the dead; not those who merely imagine themselves to be such but those who really are this kind of people and admit it.[47]

Without this understanding of who God is and what He can do for the contrite sinner, the faithful continued to believe that it was "on them" to will themselves upright. In the century leading up to Luther's ministry, "an anguished conscience had . . . become a 'mass phenomenom' in the Latin world.' Coupled with this was a piety of relentless introspection and self-examination, exhibited most clearly in the realm of monastic perfectionism."[48] In the monastic ideal, Luther saw not only a challenge to reconciling justification by faith with a vertical *curvatus* model but a revelation of a startling form of *incurvatus in se*: man whose desire to please and emulate God becomes so all-consuming that it is itself sinful. "We sin even when we do good,"[49] Luther instructs—not only the average man who longs for a pat on the back for helping a neighbor, but the monk who goes days without food, years without human contact, all with the hope of being singled out as the best, most religious man who ever walked the earth—in other words, a prideful man, a sinful man, a man curved in on his own self-centered desire. Luther notes that Isaiah 2: 9-22 "describes man as so turned in on himself that he uses not only physical but even spiritual goods for his own purposes and in all things seeks only himself."[50] He goes on to assert that "the curvedness is now natural for us, a natural wickedness and a natural sinfulness,"[51] no less experienced or expressed by those who appear closest to the divine ideal.

The zeal of monasticism was, according to Luther, not only dangerous theologically, but practically. If the highest goal of man was to live in celibate isolation, the children of God were far less likely to reproduce—not only a fatalistic stance but, more importantly, a rejection of our call to "be fruitful and multiply" (Gen 1:28a). If the monastic lifestyle was seen as the highest and best expression of the faith—a standard that none, according to Luther, could ever live up to—then ours would quickly become a Christianity of despair, as the phenomena of the "anguished conscience" was already attesting. If man's concupiscent asceticism led him to subsist on crumbs of bread and salt, then God's good Creation—the peaches and figs and honey and fishes and even the fatted calf— were all for naught. God had created them for our good use, for our good pleasure. Augustine had exhorted us to be "good users" of the lower things. Now it was Luther's call to turn the curve away from the heavens and towards the good things of this earth—to the blessings of food, air, sunshine and beauty, to be sure, but above all, to each other. This is the heart of Luther's turn from the vertical to the horizontal: a curve from our own navels to the hearts of our neighbors.

Certainly we can see in our own anatomy that we were created for interdependence. When Scripture says in

Genesis that God made for Adam a companion, he uses a word *('ezer)* that translates poorly into English as "helper." The Hebrew connotation of the word *'ezer* is "the one who does for us what we cannot do for ourselves, the one who meets our needs."[52] The verse reaffirms this complementary role with the use of the term *k'negdo*, which defines Adam's partner as not only "other" but, a "counterpart," or one that is "fit for" or "corresponding."[53] Even before we were sinners, we were incomplete in that we needed the guidance, support, love, and gifts of another (or others) to become fully human.

For years science has depicted the Garden tale as foolishness—just as many Christians have argued that the doctrine of Original Sin is passé[54]—but stay tuned: "Twenty-first century murmurings among scientists to the effect that there seems to be one common female ancestor for all human survivors of evolution"[55] may lead us one day soon to "discover" that Eve has been at the heart of the human story all along. Without this link of our shared capacity for both love and sinfulness, we "break up the race of mankind into a multitude of isolated atoms, touching, but not really connected with, one another, instead of contemplating it as one great organic whole."[56] Stripped of relationships, reduced to little more that bytes of information, hertz of productivity, decimal points of worth, our lives lose all meaning. We become detached from "the grand narrative of humanity"[57] and fall into despair.

By contrast, consider this model of one man and one woman writ large: millions of people "needing" to be made whole, and the cruel irony that our fulfillment is being thwarted by the simple, sinful act of *homo incurvatus in se*—our own and others. If only we would turn outward, we could become authentically human. We could help make our neighbors—and in the process, ourselves—complete. "The struggle in man is therefore not a struggle between a higher and lower part of man's nature, but between man's real self and the Spirit of God."[58]

If Luther were to create a continuum of physical motions that reflected his views on incurvature, and how the reversal can lead to the healing of the 'great organic whole,' it would be this: 1) man turned in on himself—the tight, fetal, sin-nursing ball; 2) man becoming pliable as clay in the hands of the potter,[59] a feat which is possible only through Christ; and 3) man yielding as Christ turns him entirely outward—from *incurvatus in se* to *excurvatus ex se*[60]. For Luther, "love they neighbor as yourself" (Matt 19:10, Lev. 19:18) is far more radical than the idea that "both the neighbor and one's own self are to be loved."[61] Rather, we are "to love *only* [italics mine] our neighbor, using our love for ourselves as the example."[62] He defends this interpretation with the scriptural teaching that man cannot love both God and mammon. In the same way, man cannot love himself and his neighbor,[63] but must love his neighbor only.

Everything about this is counterintuitive. Our natures cry out that God should either let us love ourselves perfectly well and in a way that pleases Him, or, if that is not possible, that he should turn us quickly into perfect, neighbor-loving spirits with no itch or tug to be anything else. But it can never be so. Because "sin is not localized somewhere within us, but rather *we* are sinners, it cannot be removed"[64] like pus from an abscess.

> This life, then, is a life of being healed from sin, it is not a life of sinlessness, with the cure completed and perfect health attained. The church is the inn and the infirmary for those who are sick and in need of being made well. But heaven is the palace of the healthy and the righteous.[65]

Knowing this, Luther tells us that even with this horizontal paradigm of incurvature, we will face the same perils as we did in Augustine's vertical model, where the hyper-religious were no longer acting on God's will but rather on their own desire. Love of neighbor has two equally slippery slopes: love motivated by fear and love motivated by desire. We fear that if we are not kind, good, or generous to our neighbors, we will lose favor or friendship, God will punish or reject us, or, in our current pluralistic lingo, it would be "bad karma." Perhaps more insidious is love based on desire. Luther asks us to consider the first line from Psalm 116: *I love the Lord, because He hears my voice and my supplications.* In other words, we love him because he answers our prayers.

He is, in common Christian vernacular, a "slot machine God." This same sort of selfish love is what we invariably apply towards other people, which is why Luther warns that he who

> loves his neighbor on account of his money, honor, knowledge, favor, power or comfort, and does not love the same person if he is poor, lowly, unlearned, hostile, dependent or unpleasant, clearly has a hypocritical love, not a love for him, himself but a love for his neighbor's goods for his own benefit.[66]

Being truly loving to a "hostile" neighbor is simply beyond our ability outside of Christ; even in Him, we must accept that we will not be able to reach perfection in this lifetime.

Still, the "fundamental shape of the Christian life for Luther is that of free, self-giving love which is not hampered by fear or desire."[67] This is the direction in which we must curve, not only for the sake of our neighbors but, ironically, for the realization of our highest and best selves. This is the pay-off that man fails to see in his "turned away" state. He hears the call to love neighbor and instinctively flees. The part that God leaves unspoken—or at least spelled out clearly for man's dull, stopped-up ears—is that this path of loving others *is* the very same path of becoming one's highest and best. It is our own personal land of milk and honey, where each gift will be fully utilized, each divot patched up, and the fissures of our broken hearts slowly mended until, on the last day, we are lifted up and made whole for eternity.

> The Church's unity and health depends on each believer living in joyful, self-giving freedom in the station (which would include particular gifts the Spirit gives) in which God has placed her. Vocation actually discovers, or confers grace.[68]

Despite the clear blessings of vocation (which will be discussed at length in Chapter 3), our sinful selves bristle at the perceived loss of free will. Rather than have the life that God intends for us, we turn away, "set ourselves up as judge"[69] and "exchange the truth about God for a lie" (Romans 1:25). Sin dictates desire, which leads man to fancy himself in any number of grand positions. In Luther's day, that might have meant longing to be a king or a baron or the priest in a wealthy parish. In 21st-century America, it usually translates into dreams of being a pop singing sensation, a technology superstar, or a man who makes millions on Wall Street. With vainglorious, self-selected, and ultimately thwarted "callings" such as these, "most of us are of a mind that makes us dissatisfied with our own lot. Those who are suited for a job dislike it, and the incompetent pant for it."[70]

Just as he exposed, at the one extreme, the sinful nature of monastic zeal,[71] so too Luther expanded the notion of vocation to include the life and calling of the mother, the farmhand, and the young boy who sings not for man's glory but the glory of God.[72] "Those who are unfit longing to do just what they cannot and should not do"[73] is a symptom of disordered desire, of man using "lower things" badly, or too excess.

As we move forward, remember the *incurvatus* images that Augustine and Luther have provided. We will see them undergirding the epidemic of anxiety, depression and apathy in our nation. We will see them in our rejection of the grace of vocation and the fissures between genders and classes. We will see them, unmistakably, in our growing preference for virtual relationships. In fact, the more we examine the brokenness of modern American society, the more we'll see that the breaks are born not of hard, brittle snaps, but rather of slow, steady, irresistible curves.

chapter 2

homo incurvatus in se
in the 21st- century american

When the Puritan John Winthrop set foot on American soil in 1630, he proclaimed,

> we must delight in each other, make others'
> conditions our own, rejoys together, mourn
> together, labor and suffer together, always having
> before our eyes our community as members of the
> same body.[74]

By 1772, the focus of the colonies had shifted to one of equal rights and the good life for all, with Ben Franklin declaring that in New England "every man" is a property owner, "has a Vote in public Affairs, lives in a tidy, warm House, has plenty of good Food and Fuel, with whole clothes from Head to Foot, the Manufacture perhaps of his own family."[75] By the time our forefathers drafted the Declaration of Independence, the political system bore little resemblance to Winthrop's communal "city upon the hill."[76] The document's most defining line asserted the unalienable rights of the individual and set the stage for America to become the most individualistic culture in the world.[77] Fifty-plus years later, the term *individualism* was coined by Alexis de Tocqueville to express the mindset unique to the new American democracy. He described a

> calm and considered feeling that disposes each citizen to isolate himself from the mass of his fellows and withdraw into the circle of family and friends: with this little society formed to his taste, he gladly leaves the greater society to look after itself . . . such folk owe no man anything and hardly expect anything from anybody. They form the habit of thinking of themselves in isolation and imagine that their whole destiny is in their hands.[78]

Although the Declaration of Independence acknowledges a Creator, there seems to be little reference to the Divine plan for the "tie of kinship" that Augustine described, or Winthrop had hoped for. There is surely no hint of the spirit Luther expressed when he said the Divine call was to love one's neighbor *more* than oneself. In fact, if Tocqueville's assessments were correct, America's claim as a Christian nation would be most accurate in the sense that it is a nation of Christian sinners, turned in on its own individual desires and empowered by law to pursue those desires to the full. With the same certainty that St. Paul writes, "the wages of sin is death" (Romans 6:23), Tocqueville predicted that a future built on such "radical individualism"[79] can only lead to a nation of people "constantly circling around in pursuit of the petty and banal pleasures with which they glut their souls. Each one of them, withdrawn into himself, is almost unaware of the fate of the rest."[80]

Despite the great gifts of initiative and creativity that an individualistic culture can yield, the very real downside is a citizen trained "to think of all things in terms of himself and to prefer himself to all."[81] And so, with *E Pluribus Unum* on its seal and *homo incurvatus in se* in its heart, America grew up, making its choice of masters.

In the 1980s, sociologist Robert Bellah revisited Tocqueville's field study with a new examination of American "values and aspirations."[82] He found a diverse nation of modern individualists who shunned "conformity, commitment, and obligation . . . preferring to define their own standards and do as they please."[83] He also witnessed people who defined "personality, achievement, and the purpose of human life in ways that leave the individual suspended in glorious, but terrifying, isolation."[84] As we consider the manifestations of *homo incurvatus in se* in the life of the 21st-century American, we should neither be shocked nor disappointed to find them so rampant. Turning in on ourselves is, it seems, written into our nation's charter.

how the modern american
turns in on himself:
a brief overview

Were Augustine to walk through malls of America he would come face to face with *concupiscentia* gone amok. Such is our disordered desire for "lower things." Shoes and purses and berry-scented balms; entertainment systems that overshadow our ordinary lives with escapist fantasies; toys purchased in such abundance that larger homes are needed with playrooms just to store them; the blessings of a day of gratitude scrapped for the frenzy of consumerism known, ironically, as Black Friday. Making good on Tocqueville's vision of souls glutting on "petty and banal pleasures," Americans were predicted to spend over $370 million on 2012's Halloween costumes— for their pets![85]

Move along to the mall's Food Court, and one is faced with three separate manifestations of *homo incurvatus in se* in relationship to the basic human need to eat. 1) *Obesity*. America is by far the most obese nation in the world. In 2012, 35.7% of adults and 16.5% of children were considered obese.[86] Defenses about genetics, medical conditions, and poor neighborhood options will only go so far until one is left with the simple truth: many in the United States have a disordered desire for food. 2) *Eating Disorders*. While some can't seem to eat enough, 10 million plus American women—mainly teenagers—[87]are starving themselves in the hopes of creating a body more like the media ideal, a body that will look better in the tight jeans they see at the mall. This disordered desire for an idealized physical perfection perpetually turns people in on their own obsession and away from the simple pleasures of enjoying food with family and friends. 3) *Hunger*. While many have the option of eating too much or too little, nearly 15% of U.S. households were food insecure at least some time during the year. This may or may not reflect any sort of incurvature of their own, but it clearly reflects a society that has curved away from its weaker members. "If liberals underestimate the motivating power of self-interest, conservatives underestimate sin—the selfishness that curbs the altruism needed to care for the poor."[88] This selfishness is an offshoot of the disordered desire for wealth and creature comforts—better known as greed—which fuels and is then refueled by greedy social structures e.g. "tax laws that favor large corporations"[89] and "the breathtaking salaries of CEOs."[90] As disordered desire knows no limits—and if society refuses to set them—"unseemly" displays become the new standard:

> Unseemliness is television producer Aaron Spelling building a house of 56,500 square feet and 123 rooms. Unseemliness is Henry McKinnell, the CEO of Pfizer, getting a $99 million golden parachute and an $82 million pension after a tenure that saw Pfizer's share price

plunge. They did nothing illegal. . . . But the outcomes were inappropriate for time or place, not suited to the circumstances.[91]

"The heart wants what the heart wants,"[92] Americans shrug, as if desire is its own entitlement. And how could they not? In the 1990s, there was little talk of the common good or being "thy brother's keeper" in the public space. Rather, individualistic psychologists had begun classifying people who nurtured troubled friends or family members as having the psychological disorder of being co-dependent[93] and encouraged Americans to value their own needs, desires, and personal interests over all else[94]—these were the keys to high self-esteem and a happy, successful life.[95]

For many, it seems, their greatest desire was for sex—unrestricted and consequence-free. Where our earliest forefathers would have started the day with The Lord's Prayer, by 1969—the end of the decade that launched The Pill[96]—the "cult prayer" of America was this

> I do my thing, and you do your thing.
> I am not in this world to live up
> to your expectations,
> And you are not in this world
> to live up to mine.
> You are you and I am I,
> And if by chance we find

each other, it's beautiful.

If not, it can't be helped.[97]

"Claiming to be wise, they became fools" (Romans 1:22). "For this reason, God gave them up to degrading passions" (Romans 1:26). And so the era of "if it feels good, do it" gave birth to a new generation. Unprepared to pass on any abiding wisdom about love, sex, or commitment, these "free love" adults went on to raise children without the cultural norms of "waiting for marriage" or what "good girls don't" do. Their children then grew and had kids of their own, the lessons of accepted and enforced Judeo-Christian morality now two generations removed from the common culture. The country founded on religious freedom was now a place where people had no choice but to live in a world of their own curved-in creation—a world where people did what they pleased and lived in "terrifying isolation."[98] If some remnant of an individual's God-given nature began to tug at him with pangs of shame or whispers of Original truth—one that included responsibility, morality, and the greater good—pop psychology quickly assuaged him: Don't worry, be happy![99] (Ironically, this popular ditty, excerpted from the teachings of an Indian mystic, includes both personal responsibility *and* a divine master: "Do your best. Then, don't worry; be happy in My love. I will help you").

And so by the dawn of the 21st century, the land of the brave had become the land of reaping what we sow;[100] a nation in which fellatio (not considered by most teens to be "real sex") is the "signature sex act" of teenage girls,[101] 45% of high school students are sexually active,[102] 46% of American voters—and 59% of Millennial voters—are in favor of gay marriage,[103]and, "for the first time in human history . . . a group consisting of a lone woman and her offspring is not considered to be sociologically incomplete."[104]

Promiscuity, consumerism, obesity, narcissism, apathy, greed—these are just a few of the obvious displays of *homo incurvatus in se* in 21st-century America. These behaviors—or the consequences of them—are visible and often public. Even apathy is on display by the very lack of people showing up to meet a given need. But from a pastoral or evangelistic perspective, attempting to point to any one of these behaviors as "sin," quickly becomes a case of "Do not judge someone because they sin differently than you."[105] One man's Armani suit is another's pound of fudge. And besides, the accused will snap, "who is it hurting?" This common deflection reveals what C.S. Lewis began noting as early as 1940: modern man has lost all sense that his sinful behavior is worthy of God's wrath.[106] That internalized check-and-balance between one's behavior and the Creator's response has been phased out by one hundred years where

we have so concentrated on one of the virtues— kindness or mercy—that most of us do not feel anything except kindness to be really good or anything but cruelty to be really bad. . . . The real trouble is that 'kindness' is a quality fatally easy to attribute to ourselves on quite inadequate grounds. Everyone *feels* benevolent if nothing happens to be annoying him at the moment. Thus a man easily comes to console himself for all his other vices by a conviction that 'his heart is in the right place' and 'he wouldn't hurt a fly', though in fact he has never made the slightest sacrifice for a fellow creature.[107]

As a result of our obliviousness to sin, "Christianity now has to preach the diagnosis—in itself very bad news—before it can win a hearing for the cure."[108] The diagnosis might be helped along by looking more closely at three of the shockingly common individual— and often hidden— sufferings that plague the modern American in the 21st century: **anxiety, depression,** and **a disordered relationship to technology**. Whether alone or in combination, these conditions are often at the heart of—or, in the case of technology, undergirding—the more overt expressions of *homo incurvatus in se* such as promiscuity, addiction, gluttony, consumerism, and greed.

In the sub-sections to follow, consideration will be given to each of these three conditions and how they relate to *homo incurvatus in se* in the following ways: 1) Man turns away from God and toward his own desires

44

because he wants to be his own God. Now, if you or I were the only soul on earth—as our narcissism often deludes us into thinking— this problem would be manageable. But a world filled with creatures *each* trying to be his own God quickly leads to chaos: if everyone is in charge, no one is in charge. This ever-mutating, self-created chaos "bounces back" to the modern man in the form of increasing anxiety and depression. 2) Our self-centeredness turns our fellow man into our competition. "If, being cowardly, conceited and slothful, you have never yet done a fellow creature great mischief, that is only because your neighbor's welfare has not yet happened to conflict with your safety, self-approval, or ease. Every vice leads to cruelty."[109] This "zero-sum" mentality leads to greater distrust, which, in turn, "justifies" our curving ever more inward. 3) We are social creatures in a world that now feels chaotic and untrustworthy. We therefore create "safe" and undemanding simulations of community for ourselves through technology. Online we can all be our own Gods (we can even imagine we've recreated the "bonds of kinship") as the virtual/digital life pulls us deeper into the "journey homeward to habitual self."[110] With that, we now look more closely at anxiety, depression, and our disordered relationship to technology.

anxiety

The DSM-IV criteria for anxiety disorder includes "at least six months of excessive worry," "tension, fatigue, trouble concentrating, sleeplessness," and "clinically significant distress functioning in daily life."[111] Merriam Webster includes in the definition for anxiety, "doubt concerning the reality and nature of the threat and . . . self-doubt about one's capacity to cope with it."[112] Soren Kierkegaard—whose existential philosophy focuses on how one lives as a "single individual"[113]—uses metaphor to express the truths of anxiety:

> Anxiety may be compared with dizziness. He whose eye happens to look down into the yawning abyss becomes dizzy. But what is the reason for this? It is just as much in his own eye as in the abyss, for suppose he had not looked down. Hence anxiety is the dizziness of freedom, which emerges when the spirit . . . looks down into its own possibility, laying hold of finiteness to support itself. Freedom succumbs in this dizziness.[114]

Pastor Robert W. Kellemen, by contrast, claims that anxiety is simply "fear without faith."[115] Each of these definitions provides insight into this alarming trend in American mental illness. Since 1980, reported anxiety disorders in the U.S. have increased 1,200%.[116] A 1994 study, which asked a random sample of thousands of Americans about their mental health, revealed 15% who'd suffered from anxiety disorders. Fifteen years later, a similar study found nearly half of the sample—as many as 117 million U.S. adults—had experienced at some point anxiety severe enough to meet the standards for a disorder.[117] Of particular concern for the nation's future well being are several studies that reveal "a significant increase in anxiety levels in children and college students."[118] This is compared to the emotional well being of kids, teens, and young adults fifty years ago.[119] "If progress is measured in the mental health and happiness of young people, then we have been going backward at least since the early 1950s."[120]

There might be any number of explanations for why America's youth might find the world more overwhelming than in the "good 'ol days." Before we succumb to the rose-colored lens of nostalgia, consider this: rates of anxiety and depression in young people were *far lower* during The Great Depression, World War II, The Cold War, and the tumultuous periods of social change of the 1960s and early 70s than they are today.[121] Closer examination reveals that America's increasingly anxious young people are not the by-product of "realistic dangers and uncertainties"[122] in a global society, nor do they correlate with economic cycles, wars, or life-changing world events.[123] The clearest evidence seems to suggest that children and college-aged students are more anxious than ever because they have lost the essential belief that they are in control of their own destinies.[124] Dr. Jean Twenge observes that "Generation Me"—those born in the 1970s, 80s, and 90s —may be "tolerant, confident, open-minded, and ambitious" but they are also "cynical, depressed, lonely, and anxious."[125] Growing up in the mall, and in a "bling-saturated" media culture, they could not help but develop a disordered desire for "stuff." Coming to terms with just how much the latest "stuff" costs, as well as being on the receiving end of relentless messaging about the type of education and career success that is expected of them, has created a seismic undercurrent for anxiety. Perhaps that's why, during the coming-of-age periods for these generations, there was a marked shift from intrinsic to extrinsic goals:

> Intrinsic goals are those that have to do with one's own development as a person—such as becoming competent in endeavors of one's choosing and developing a meaningful philosophy of life. Extrinsic goals . . . are those that have to do with material rewards and other people's judgments. They include goals of high income, status, and good looks . . . young people today are, on average, more oriented toward extrinsic goals and less oriented toward intrinsic goals than they were in the past.[126]

How is it that focusing on extrinsic goals has made young people feel less in control and more anxious? Twenge suggests this line of thinking:

> To the extent that my emotional sense of satisfaction comes from progress toward intrinsic goals I can control my emotional wellbeing. To the extent that my satisfaction comes from others'

48

judgments and rewards, I have much less control
over my emotional state.[127]

In the language of *homo incurvatus in se* we would say
that a disordered desire for admiration, power, wealth,
success or desirability—extrinsic goals— leads one to
"turn in" on a warped path of self. Although the term
"intrinsic goal" may sound more like the action of turning
inward, what it actually represents is turning one's ear
toward an understanding of who one is and what one
believes, namely, to focus one's development such that
he "will know the truth and the truth will set them free"
(John 7: 32). This process of coming to know one's true
self rarely follows the strict "test-taking, GPA-boosting,
resume-building timetable" that extrinsic benchmarks
require. Time spent with friends relaxing means time not
spent cramming for an AP exam. Taking up an activity
such as skateboarding or hiking or gardening—without
the "admissions bump" of being the president of the club
or including underprivileged kids in the mix—becomes a
luxury for the truly goal-oriented young adult.

But ambition is nothing new. Why then would
21st-century Americans—young and old alike—find it
bringing them to such an anxious state? The answer
would appear to be two-fold.

**we've come to equate our extrinsic goals with
the pursuit of happiness**

As soon as an American baby is born, its parents enter into an implicit contractual obligation to answer any question about their hopes for their tiny offspring's future with the words: "I don't care, as long as he's happy" (the mental suffix "at Harvard" must remain unspoken). Happiness in America has become the overachiever's ultimate trophy. A vicious trump card, it outranks professional achievement and social success, family, friendship and even love. Its invocation can deftly minimize others' achievements ("Well, I suppose she has the perfect job and a gorgeous husband, but is she really happy?") and take the shine off our own.[128]

Part of the blame can be placed on the self-esteem movement that swept the nation in the final years of the 20th century, creating whole households chanting the mantra, "Every day, in every way, I'm getting better and better"[129]—based on no evidence whatsoever. Where once a child who was underachieving, unpopular, unruly, or obnoxious faced painful, instructive, real-time consequences, the remedy of choice for modern children was a booster shot of self-esteem. Referring to the 2010 PISA results, which assess 15-year olds worldwide, Paul E. Peterson, director of Harvard University's Program on Education Policy and Governance noted that in mathematics, "the U.S. ranks number 1 in self-esteem and number 32 in performance."[130] Faced with a zero-sum college or job market, "specialness" is sorely tested.

When it is finally revealed that a grown child is lacking in the skills, attributes, or wherewithal to be The Best (and the parents' *raison d'etre* has not turned out as spectacularly as they had hoped), anxiety is inevitable:

> This obsessive, driven, relentless pursuit [of happiness] is a characteristically American struggle—the exhausting daily application of the Declaration of Independence. . . . Despite being the richest nation on earth, the United States is, according to the World Health Organization, by a wide margin, also the most anxious. . . . America's precocious levels of anxiety are not just happening in spite of the great national happiness rat race, but also perhaps, because of it.[131]

we've taken God out of the equation

In doing so, we have robbed ourselves and our children of the security of knowing our place in the world. Kierkegaard, the father of "existential angst," often uses the words from the Gospel of Matthew 16:26:

> 'For what is a man profited, if he shall gain the whole world, and lost his own soul?' To lose ourselves is to wound our soul . . . That which we forget [or lose] is precisely that which anxiety reveals: that we are a self with the task of becoming

ourselves.[132]

In the language of *homo incurvatus in se*, this process of "becoming ourselves" is one of turning back to God. It is not hard to imagine that someone raised without any exposure to the Judeo-Christian faith would be unlikely to heed the call to "turn to me and be saved, all the ends of the earth! For I am God, and there is no other" (Isaiah 45:22). The greater problem would seem to lie with those who identify themselves as Christians, who, according to George Barna, "often fail to realize that the end game of spiritual development is godly character, not worldly accomplishments." Although 81% say they have made a personal commitment to Jesus Christ that is important in their life today, only 18% of them claims to be totally committed to investing in their own spiritual development and 22% to be "completely dependent upon God."[133] This leads the modern day Christian to "hedge their bets" with the same extrinsic goals pursued by non-believers, increasing the competition for those "brass rings" and leaving them just as susceptible to the "dizzying abysses" of anxiety.

If every "dysfunctional, fallen emotion is a distortion of God's original, pre-fall design,"[134] a better understanding of the problem requires we identify the "normal, healthy, God-given process [that] has become disturbed in anxiety."[135]

God placed Adam in the garden 'to work it and

take care of it' (Genesis 2:15). The KJV says 'to dress it and to keep it.' The Hebrew word behind 'take care of' and 'keep' means 'to guard, protect, keep safe, watch over, keep vigil.' God built into our brains a sentry, a sentinel . . . Vigilance is the proper, constructive concern for the well-being of others and for the advancement of God's Kingdom.[136]

Anxiety, then, is vigilance that has lost sight of God.[137] It is the reflection of our desperate attempts to "go it alone," refusing to believe that we can't do just as good a job with our lives as God can—better even. This self-driven approach demands affirmation in the form of visible and impressive extrinsic accomplishments, and leaves us face to face with our very real and human limitations. When, by contrast, we turn back to God, He helps lead us daily towards our intrinsic selves. These selves are then revealed *in His time* in any number of extrinsic manifestations, which may or may not impress anyone, but will wholly and joyfully fulfill our individual sense of self and purpose—our "room" in the "Father's house."

Martin Luther, who struggled mightily with anxiety, believed that one cannot deal with life's daily fears without first making peace with life's ultimate fear—death.[138] If Luther is right, then America is not getting any closer to the target. In today's narcissistic culture, man seeks not to inflict his own certainties on others but to find meaning in life . . . The contemporary climate is therapeutic, not religious. People today hunger not for personal salvation, let alone the restoration of an earlier golden age, but for the feeling, the momentary illusion, of personal well-being.[139]

As long as Americans continue to pursue that well-being without turning back to God, anxiety will continue to metastasize. Businesses seem to be banking on it. In the fall of 2012, the Pharmaceutical Research and Manufacturers of America issued a report touting the many new drugs being developed for mental illness. Twenty-six of them were for anxiety.[140]

The society that we believed we understood and in which we felt secure during the 1950s has become incomprehensible and threatening in the 21st century. Our level of trust of authority, from religion through medicine to politics, has declined dramatically. . . . Though much of our trust in the past was misplaced, our more accurate view of society has lead to what some call "the gravest sort of anxiety." Such anxiety results from a sense that we have lost our foundations and that chaos reigns. Chaos and its resultant anxiety cannot be tolerated for long, and depression, a signal to withdraw, is perhaps a natural adaptation to these feelings.[141]

depression

Anxiety and depression are "fraternal twins."[142] Close to 50% of those who suffer from anxiety disorder will develop major depression within five years.[143] Depression is the leading cause of disability worldwide, and is a major contributor to the global burden of disease.[144] Many experts feel it has reached a state of epidemic.[145] Twenty years ago, about 1.5% of the U.S. population had a level of depression that required treatment; today, as many as 50% can expect to experience depression's symptoms.[146]

Any discussion of depression in the context of religion—particularly in the context of sin—is potentially volatile. Within the religious community there is dissension about the relationship between depression and faith. Many struggle to understand why God would allow depression in the first place[147] while others chide—much like Job's friends—that the depressed Christian must be doing something wrong. Some insist it's a sin to use medication to treat depression—that only Christ can heal what is, in effect, a spiritual problem—others that it's a sin *not* to use medication when tangible help is available. After all, "Jesus told his disciples that he had come to Earth so that they should have more joy and have it completely."[148] Twelfth-century mystic, Hildegard of Bingen, contended, "At the moment when Adam disobeyed the divine law, at that exact instant, melancholy coagulated in his blood."[149] Contemporary writer and Christian, Kathleen Norris, takes a peacemaker's role. "Depression has many causes: genetic disposition and chemical imbalance in the brain, as well as unwelcome change, notably loss in all its forms. Can we agree that there are many treatments as well?"[150]

Because the landscape is so vast, for the purposes of this short section the focus will be on 1) how the acceleration in cases of major depression parallels the trend in modern psychiatry away from a consideration of social context to a purely individualistic model; and 2) the individual's experience of depression and how it relates to their connection to God. Let's begin with a view from 10,000 feet.

Over the past 50 years, those tasked as healers in the field of depression have abandoned examination of society's role and placed the focus wholly on the individual, both in cause and solution. Since this might leave the individual stigmatized, depression was then re-envisioned as a one-size-fits-many disease[151] for which the person is not responsible. The cure is a pill, and, for the most part, the pill works[152]—problem solved—which makes it less likely that experts will ever go back to looking for the social causes behind the problem. The arc is eerily similar to the pattern we've followed in removing "sin" from the public square. First we made it an individual act (as opposed to a condition that applied to all mankind). Then, so that the sinner is not stigmatized, we decided that this act or that was no longer a sin—problem solved—and that, really, sin doesn't even exist anymore. We've conquered it. And yet our sickness grows.

considering the social context

In the first half of the 20th century, there was increasing concern in both general medicine and psychiatry about the social and cultural contributions to mental illness.[153] "To treat depression, one must treat a depressogenic society,"[154] it was felt, which led to the creation of the Community Mental Health Center movement in the 1960s. Despite a strong vision, it was soon recognized that psychiatry and government were "inept"[155] at treating the ills of the culture and there was a speedy and almost universal retreat from considering the "implications of a potentially noxious society."[156]

> This lack of interest in the social origins of depression reflects the tendency to attribute depression (and virtually all illnesses) to causes that can, in theory, be controlled by the individual or by interventions directed toward the individual. This person-specific, concrete approach undoubtedly reflects our highly individualistic society, coupled with a loss of confidence that we can effect society-wide social changes.[157]

Individuals do not seek help because they are concerned about an ailing society. Their personal concerns are the ordinary sufferings of everyday life—sex, marriage, worldly failures.[158] For the past 2000 years, these issues of the human condition have fallen under the realm of the church—the Body of Christ on earth, born of His suffering and created to heal mankind through grace. Somehow, in the second half of the 20th century, the "balm of Gilead" was proving insufficient for the pain of the modern era. Perhaps a Christmas & Easter faith (and certainly, no faith at all) is not strong enough to weather hard times. Or perhaps the church, turned in on its own need for affirmation through lively and ever-increasing attendance, shirked its duties to preach the theology of the Cross. Either way, as Michael Norden suggests in *Beyond Prozac,* it's no longer relevant whether individual genes or biology or society (or, I might add, shallow faith or teaching) has caused the problems: the problems are real and universal.[159]

> As the world we live in has changed drastically over centuries and millennia, the human body and brain have remained virtually the same. We have yet to develop the necessary coping mechanisms to deal with the alarming stresses of our modern technology era [so] we medicate, using everything from caffeine to Prozac. Modern living, from stress on the job to the air we breathe, has led to depletion of the brain's serotonin . . . Prozac-like drugs were designed to bolster our weakened

neurochemical "stress shield" by increasing the serotonin levels in the brain.[160]

This may be true, but it ignores two essential facts: 1) less stressed, less-depressed individuals do not automatically make better, healthier societies, and 2) Jesus Christ promised to be with us "til the end of the age" (Matthew 28:20). This means that He is with us even if our serotonin gets depleted, and we turn further in on our own sinful natures, and we find a thousand ways to try to solve the problem without Him. The 21st–century dilemma, therefore, begins with the paradigm of the Garden: we are meant to be in healthy relationship to God and to one another. For all the good works of modern psychiatry, it has, unfortunately, "found the brain but lost the person within his or her family and community."[161]

the depressed individual and God

The term *depression* was likely first used in 1761 when Samuel Johnson wrote that he felt "a dejection, gloom, and despair, which made existence misery"[162] and was "under a great depression."[163] Before that, the condition was usually referred to as *melancholia,* which was often closely related to spiritual and religious practices.[164] Throughout the Middle Ages and into the Renaissance, there were several ways that *melancholia* was interpreted. The cause "might be direct from God as punishment for sin, direct from God for self-improvement as a purge of sins, or abandonment by God to the devil or demons."[165] In the early days of the desert fathers, this pressed-down feeling was described using the Greek root word for the "absence of care"—*acedia*—[166]which was once one of the Eight Deadly Sins. The term later disappeared, collapsed into Sloth.[167] Although a difficult concept to pin down, Thomas Aquinas distilled it to "aversion of the appetite from its own good," specifically an "aversion against God himself. . . . It is the opposite of joy in the divine good that [we] should experience."[168]

> As we languish from spiritual drought, we are often unaware of what ails us. We spend greater sums on leisure but are more tense than ever, and hire lifestyle coaches to ease the stress. We turn away from the daily news, complaining of "compassion fatigue," and enroll in classes to learn now to breathe and relax. Increasingly, we need drugs in order to sleep. We are tempted to regard with reverence those dedicated souls who make themselves available "twenty-four/seven" and regard silence as unproductive, solitude as irresponsible. But when distraction becomes the norm, we are in danger of becoming immunized from feeling itself. We are more likely to indulge in public spectacles of undemanding pseudo-care than address humanity's immediate needs. Is it possible that in twenty-first-century America, acedia has come into its own?[169]

With acedia—and its modern day sister, depression—we

become apathetic and numb. Medication may treat the sensations of depression but the numbness remains because the numbness is not biological, but spiritual.[170] Much like the cure of soma in Aldous Huxley's *Brave New World*, we have solved the individual's problem of surviving the day but numbed ourselves to the big picture.[171] According to John N. Blackwell, 21st-century Americans are suffering from "a kind of sleeping sickness that includes indifference, apathy, and joylessness."[172] We refuse to call it sin. We refuse to contemplate the context of our depressed states, treating the symptoms while ignoring the cause. But alone in the dark each night the truth of our suffering cries out:

> Everyone I know is lonely/
> And God's so far away/
> And my heart belongs to no one/
> So now some times I pray
> Please take this space between us/
> And fill it up some way[173]
>
> —Sting

We have noted that anxiety is the disordered state of God-given vigilance. What then are we to make of depression? What God-pleasing good is the flipside of this suffering? "Depression is the flaw in love. To be creatures who love, we must be creatures who can despair at what we lose, and depression is the mechanism of that despair."[174] Those who do not know God, suffer the loss of that One great love. As Pastor Marc Brown teaches,

"Depression is not a sign of weakness but a reminder that we need God."[175] For those who already know the risen Lord, depression may be a call to grow closer.

> A full insight into the hopelessness and inescapability of our situation is the first real fruit of the purgative night. Even our most sincere attempts at self-transcendence are colored with self. It is only in the full experience of our bind, of the impossibility of self-help at this level, that we are reduced to genuine humility and prepared for grace.[176]

What was true for countless desert fathers and the father of "the dark night of the soul," St. John of the Cross,"[177] is still true today: the Christian is as susceptible to depression as the non-believer. "Even those people whose faith promises them that this will all be different in the next world cannot help experiencing anguish in this one: Christ himself was the man of sorrows."[178]

The remedy the man of sorrows has given us in simple: "Love the lord your God with all your heart, soul, and mind, and love your neighbor as yourself." In our refusal to heed His words, and our perpetual preference for a state of *homo incurvatus in se*, Americans have rendered themselves sick with joylessness, "even in the face of extraordinary goodness and love."[179]

a disordered relationship
to technology

In some ways the story begins with the curse of Genesis 3: 17-19 and modern man's efforts to free himself from that toil. With each new technological innovation, leisure time has been increased leaving people at a loss for how to spend it. With the advent of television, a technology that proliferated throughout American households faster than any before it,[180] the trend toward "cocooning"—a cozy name for the sin of turning in on one's own creature comforts—flourished. By the 1970s, a profound cross-fade of activity was underway as families started spending more time at home, specifically watching TV, and less time going out with friends or relatives for a meal, a visit, or some shared entertainment.[181] As T.S. Eliot observed presciently in the early years of television, "It is a medium of entertainment which permits million of people to listen to the same joke at the same time, and yet remain lonesome."[182] By 2013, the average American watched 5 hours and 11 minutes of TV per day.[183] There is little disagreement that the American addiction to television viewing has far-reaching negative consequences:

> Television is the cheapest and least demanding way of averting boredom. Studies of television find that of all household activities, television requires the lowest level of concentration, alertness, challenge and skill … viewers are prone

to habituation, desensitization, and satiation.[184]

As our earlier explanations of the consequences of *homo incurvatus in se* would predict, excessive television viewing is detrimental to real social connectedness:

> Television as a medium creates a false sense of companionship, making people *feel* intimate, informed, clever, busy, and important . . . viewers *feel* engaged with our community without the effort of actually *being* engaged. . . . Like junk food, TV, especially entertainment, satisfies cravings without any real nourishment.[185]

Since 99% of American households have at least one television, some wisdom might be found from the 1%—which include the Amish of eastern Pennsylvania—about why one might choose to shun this technology:

> We can almost always tell if a change will bring good or bad tidings. Certain things we definitely do not want, like the television and the radio. They would destroy our visiting practices. We would stay at home with the television or radio rather than meet with other people. . . . How can we care for the neighbor if we do not visit them or know what is going on in their lives?[186]

Ironically, the story of television's sway as the "800-pound gorilla of leisure time"[187] seems almost quaint in light of the technological revolutions of the early 21st century. For the purposes of this thesis, the remaining focus in this brief section will be limited to how technology is changing the way future generations view "relationships" vis a vis social media, online and video gaming, and the ever-increasing reality of relationships with "creatures" through artificial intelligence, namely, robots.

In 2012, 69% of all internet users—and 92% of those aged 18-29—were engaged in social media.[188] Unlike with television, experts have mixed feelings about whether or not this new form of socializing is a good thing. A 2006 study suggested that "the social ties supported by these technologies are relatively weak and geographically dispersed, not the strong, often locally-based ties that tend to be a part of peoples' core discussion network."[189] A 2010 Pew Forum study contradicted those studies. It claimed instead that

> Americans are not as isolated as has been previously reported. People's use of the mobile phone and the internet is associated with larger and more diverse discussion networks. And, when we examine people's full personal network—their strong and weak ties—internet use in general and use of social networking services such as Facebook in particular are associated with more diverse social networks.[190]

As with all complex questions regarding new technologies and human life, there is not yet consensus about whether the upsides outweigh the down.

Where there is little disagreement, however, is that the one-on-one relationship between computer and user has morphed into a new, virtual reality of "so-called" friends. "We [are] no longer limited to a handful of close friends and contacts [but] could have hundreds, even thousands, a dazzling breadth of connection."[191] What MySpace (2003) began, Facebook (2004) writ large, and Twitter, Pinterest, Blogger, Instagram, and Tumbler continue to build on has created a new frontier where consumers now spend more time on social networks than on any other site.[192] This represents "a 37 percent increase in the total time spent on social media in the U.S.,"[193] in the past year alone. "It is so ingrained and has touched every facet of everything we do all day long. We are literally taking our phones with us to the bathroom and connecting on social media."[194] How can it be that this new virtual world order reflects incurvature when people are using these networks to interact with others?

> These days, insecure in our relationships and anxious about intimacy, we look to technology for ways to be in relationships and protect ourselves from them at the same time. . . . We fear the risk and disappointments of relationships with our fellow humans. We expect more from technology and less from each other.[195]

There is also the very real problem—especially for teens—that the images people project on social media sites are not an accurate picture.

> Creating a profile in a friend-networking site necessarily entails some degree of impression management . . . which can create pressure on teens and children to present themselves in the best light possible. The need to belong to groups and pressure to conform to stereotypes can play a part in forming one's identity both online and offline. Adolescents' self-esteem is also affected by the type of feedback received on their profiles, with positive feedback increasing self-esteem and negative feedback decreasing self-esteem.[196]

This feedback loop can become both anxiety-provoking and irresistible,[197] even beyond the high school years. In a recent study of college freshman, 48% of the girl strongly agree/agreed that they sometimes felt addicted to Facebook,[198] 75% said they knew someone who was addicted to Facebook,[199] and "almost a third of females wished they didn't have the 'need' to be on Facebook."[200] This would seem to echo Augustine's thought that "the point was for man to be his own king, to have everything to himself under his own control; but he finds that his grasp for autonomy has led to slavery."[201]

Real life is not conducted asynchronously nor does it include only exciting, delightful, newsworthy, or telegenic moments. By creating social media facades that project only what one wants to project—and communicating only when and where one chooses—young users are turning in more on their desire to look good to others, even as they wonder, "to what degree . . . followers are . . . friends."[202] This element of creating a "false self" can be even more problematic in online and video gaming, where one creates avatars and participates in make-believe worlds. The experience can give the impression of being fully satisfying until

> after an evening of avatar-to-avatar talk in a networked game, we feel, at one moment, in possession of a full social life and, in the next, curiously isolated, in tenuous complicity with strangers. . . . Creating an avatar . . . is a way to explore the self. But if you're spending three, four, or five hours a day in an online game or virtual world (a time commitment that is not unusual), there's got to be someplace you're not. And that someplace you're not is often with your family and friends—sitting around, playing Scrabble face-to-face, taking a walk, watching a movie together in the old-fashioned way. . . . You might have begun your online life in a spirit of compensation. If you were lonely and isolated, it seemed better than nothing. But online, you're slim, rich, and buffed up, and you feel you have more opportunities than in the real world. So, here, too, better than nothing can become better than

something—or better than anything. Not surprisingly, people report feeling let down when they move from the virtual to the real world.[203]

This idea of technology being better than nothing—and then somehow, better than anything—which has developed incrementally from television to the internet to gaming to social media is now leading to the widespread integration of robots into daily life.[204] "The idea of sociable robots suggests that we might navigate intimacy by skirting it. People seem comforted by the belief that if we alienate or fail each other, robots will be there, programmed to provide simulations of love."[205] As Americans are having children later and later, and the baby boomers move into old age, robots will become a viable option for tending to kids, to old people, or to anyone we simply don't have the energy for.[206] Many may feel this sounds like science fiction or something only the very young might live to see, but the future has arrived, and 1st-world cultures—especially the most individualistic of them all—seem to be more relieved than concerned:

A forty-four year old woman says, 'After all, we never know how another person feels. People put on a good face. Robots would be safer.' A thirty-year-old man remarks, 'I'd rather talk to a robot. Friends can be exhausting. The robot will always be there for me. And whenever I'm done, I can walk away.'. . . In a complicated world, robots seem a simple salvation.[207]

At the heart of this new trend is the fact that technology creates the illusion of having our needs met without having to be beholden to other people to do it. Why negotiate over which show to watch when each family member can simply go to his own screen? Why get involved with some clumsy community effort when one can practice world domination online? Why make oneself vulnerable to another person by asking for help or advice when a computer can do a better job—and with no risk of exposure?

During the mid-70s' launch of ELIZA, the first significant companion robot, Sherry Turkle observed that although the test students knew full well that ELIZA had been trained to respond to strings of words with various restatements and had no comprehension of anything they were saying, nonetheless

> they wanted to chat with it. More than this, they wanted to be alone with it. They wanted to tell it their secrets. Faced with a program that makes the smallest gesture suggesting it can empathize, people want to say something true. . . . Most commonly they begin with 'How are you today?' … but four or five interchanges later, many are on to 'My girlfriend left me,' 'I am worried that I might fail organic chemistry,' or 'My sister died.'[208]

Over the past several decades, our progressive baby steps

in turning towards technology for succor have led us to prefer confidantes who won't judge us and have no needs of their own.[209] We, like infants, want all the focus on ourselves, and the robotics movement is happy to oblige. What began with children's toys such as Furby and Zhu Zhu has now given rise to the "huggable, baby seal robot Paro"[210] being aggressively marketed as a companion for the elderly. Whereas real pets are a proven source of comfort and meaning for often-isolated seniors, these robotic companions pose serious questions. Trained to echo their owners' moods, a tender touch will cause Paro to turn sympathetically and simulate concern. An old woman appears comforted by this, but how many "generations" removed is this from the real love she once knew from her own parents, gave to her own children, heard about in the promises of a loving God. Paro is not the grown son she longs to have visit her in the senior center,[211] or even a warm-blooded pet that might actually fall into a depression after her death. Her robotic companion is a façade of love, the next best thing, her only remaining option. Experts have begun to recognize that "our willingness to engage with the inanimate does not depend on being deceived but on wanting to fill in the blanks."[212] And our societal willingness to allow machines to do the work of loving and caring for those in the human family is a reflection of the very real sin of apathy.

[This] is all too recognizable in the United States, where the term 'granny dumping' is used to define the practice of anonymously depositing our elderly on the doorsteps of nursing homes, and where urban hospitals have been known to abandon indigent patients on skid row, some still in their hospital gowns and with IVs in their arms. But even as such outrages are exposed, we are beset by a curious silence; the more that society's ills surface in such evil ways, the less able we are, it seems to detect any evil within ourselves, let alone work effectively together to fix what is wrong. The philosopher Alasdair MacIntyre finds that while our 'present age is perhaps no more evil than a number of preceding periods . . . it is evil in one special way at least, namely the extent to which we have obliterated . . . [our] consciousness of evil.[213]

If evil is systemic, cultural, and pervasive, then sin is the intimate response to that evil perpetrated by an individual in a specific and human way.[214] Often times it appears more tragic—even pitiful— than nefarious. Let us close out the chapter with the example of Howard. Like every teenage boy or girl, fifteen-year old Howard longs for advice about navigating the social challenges of adolescence.[215] He doesn't consider talking to his father because, as he sees it, his father "has knowledge of basic things, but not enough about high school."[216] Although this is merely a restatement of the timeless and universal teenage cry, "You wouldn't understand," Howard feels certain that true wisdom is possible through artificial intelligence. After all, a robot—which modern children describe as being "alive enough"[217] for their purposes—could

> monitor all of their e-mails, calls, Web searches, and messages. This machine could supplement its knowledge with its own searches and retain a nearly infinite amount of data. . . . Such search and storage and artificial intelligence . . . might tune itself to their exact needs . . . as Howard puts it, 'how different social choices have worked out.' Having knowledge and your best interest at heart, 'it would be good to talk to . . . about romantic matters. And problems of friendship.' [218]

If given a chance to talk with a companion robot, Howard claims that he would first ask "about happiness and exactly what that is, how do you gain it?" He would then seek understanding about human fallibility, and if he could learn to avoid making mistakes.[219] These used to be the lessons we learned in families, in communities, in church. In our desire to mediate the challenges of relationships, we have triangulated, putting technology in the driver's seat between two humans, and removing God from the picture entirely. The more society encourages flesh and blood needs to be met by inanimate objects, the more uncomfortable we'll become with other people— their needs, mess, weakness, yes, but so, too, their warmth, wisdom, grace, and love.

When young Howard is asked about other ways robots might be useful in the future, there is a tender and telling note of altruism. He hopes that they "might be specially trained to take care of 'the elderly and children,' something he doesn't see the people around him as much interested in.[220] It is a truth so glaring that even religious skeptics must confess that we've taken a wrong turn. "Religious conviction is largely beneficent," says biologist E.O. Wilson. "Religion . . . nourishes love, devotion, and above all, hope."[221] Psychologist William Damon adds, "Children will not thrive . . . unless they acquire a living sense of what some religious traditions have called *transcendence*: a faith in, and devotion to, concerns that are considered larger than the self."[222] In other words, the dark truths of *homo incurvatus in se* in the 21st century are apparent not only to Christians but to anyone who cares to notice.

Throughout this chapter, we have seen how each individual's turned-in state contributes to a culture that becomes more competitive and less trustworthy, exacerbating the individual's suffering. Next, we will consider how *homo incurvatus in se* harms far more than the individual, impacting the entire social fabric of America and threatening to destroy the very promise of our democracy.

chapter 3

how the *inward turned man* leads to the fracturing of human society

In Garret Hardin's 1968 essay, "The Tragedy of the Commons," he asserts that shared resources needed to sustain the life and livelihoods of a group have always been undermined—even to the point of elimination—by individuals acting in their own self-interest.[223] Hardin's premise is drawn from an 1833 pamphlet on medieval land usage which surmises that "the commons" provide plenty of grazable land for each farmer's cows, unless—or inevitably, until—each farmer decides to add a few more, and a few more still, each choosing his own gain over the clear loss to the whole, and ultimately destroying the life-giving land and grass that once sustained them all.[224] His assertions have been correlated to a wide range of theories—economic, ecological, social, evolutionary—but rarely, if ever, to sin.

The wisdom that "sin hurts the life of the whole community"[225] was once as obvious to pagans and philosophers as it was to the children of God. In the highly multicultural and pluralistic Mediterranean world of the 1st century, people were united by a common understanding that "all things come from God/gods."[226] This included rain, food, love, family, and ultimately, life. "Sinners were [considered] deviants who jeopardized"[227] everyone's shot at, not only a good life, but any life at all. The wisdom of Greek philosophy seemed to lead to the same conclusion. In Plato's *Gorgias*, Socrates makes the case that so great is the torture of unpunished sin (punishment being the corrective influence of the group), that a wise man—knowing he has acted unjustly or has done harm to another—will "run to the judge, as he would to the physician, in order that the disease of injustice may not be rendered chronic."[228] For Ancient Jews, "sin was largely communal; the Jewish community believed that united they would stand and divided they would fall."[229]

That had once been the promise and commitment of America. Today, we live as if we're "free to do what we want, any old time,"[230]regardless of our impact on "the commons." Even Christians have lost their way, opting now to think of sin "as something more personal: the idea [isn't] so much to save your community as to save yourself."[231] This radical individualism is now undermining exponentially the foundation of the freedom that made it possible.

The American project . . . consists of the

continuing effort, begun with the founding, to demonstrate that human beings can be left free as individuals and families to live their lives as they see fit, coming together voluntarily to solve their joint problems. The polity based on that idea led to a civic culture that was seen as exceptional by all the world. That culture was so widely shared among Americans that it amounted to a civil religion. . . . That culture is unraveling.[232]

Such is the price of our relentless inward turn. "When individualism is taken to an extreme, individuals become its ironic casualties."[233] And so it is that we have allowed the rich to get richer at the expense of the "ninety-nine" (Matthew 18:12) left behind—the sin of greed killing dreams, dignity, and hope. We have watched as creatures, both animal and human, have been sickened by toxic waste—death through the sin of hubris, greed, or neglect. We have shrugged as a media culture killed off our children's innocence and choked our common lives with sex, scandal, and violence. Until, in the final weeks of 2012, the murder of 26 young children and their teachers, and the mother of a troubled boy, made it clear that something is terribly wrong in America and getting worse: of the twelve deadliest shootings in U.S. history, *half* have been in the past five years.[234]

By the time this thesis is presented, we will know more about what sort of corrective, first-use-of-the-law actions the United States might take as a result of the massacre at Sandy Hook Elementary and others. The response may be helpful, but it will not be curative. Because underneath all that has gone so terribly wrong is still that single, most objectionable word: sin. While "unfathomable" events may prompt us to consider how the actions of "they" and "them" can hurt us all, we are not quite so willing to look at how the actions of "I" and "me" contribute to this collective evil.

This first-person singular will be the area of focus for this chapter— specifically, how each one of us chooses to live, love, work and contribute, and how it affects the larger society in two key areas: Marriage, and the breakdown of this essential building block of society, and Vocation, and the loss of this divine method of ordering and blessing society. In each case we will see how our propensity to turn towards our own desires, and away from the good, shared life God had planned, is at the heart of all that has gone wrong with "us."

marriage

In the year 2012, if the word "marriage" appeared in an American newspaper it was most likely in the context of either gay marriage or the decline in marriage altogether. This thesis will not devote time to the issue of gay marriage for two reasons: 1) from a biblical perspective, there is no new insight to be added about homosexual relations as a reflection of *homo incurvatus in se*, and 2) the public perception of the size and significance of this issue is highly inflated. According to a 2011 Gallup poll, "U.S. adults, on average, estimate that 25% of Americans are gay or lesbian,"[235] with the highest estimates given by those with the lowest level of education and income.[236] In actuality, only 3.5% of the U.S. population self-reports as gay, lesbian, bi-sexual, or transgender.[237] More than half of those consider themselves to be bi-sexual. Since bi-sexuals are not committed to one sex or the other they are, therefore, less likely to commit to marriage at all: if they do, there's a 50-50 chance it would be a heterosexual union. This would make the available pool of candidates for gay marriage roughly 2% of all Americans, which is statistically insignificant for the fabric of American life.

We move on, then, to the aspect of marriage that presents the greatest risk to American life: the steady decline in legal, lifelong unions between a man and a woman, typically resulting in children and the creation of a nuclear family unit. Although the Bible makes clear that the "traditional" family is God's plan for the growth, health, and stability of humanity, the case can be made compellingly without Scripture. "Pair bonding is the trademark of the human animal."[238] In ancient Greece, marriage was an essential part of civic life. Although extracurricular sexual outlets were permitted for men,[239] monogamy was strictly practiced and enforced, and unmarried men were "treated with scorn."[240] Monogamous marriage was the norm in ancient Rome, as well, where many simply "became married" by living together for a year, while others committed to elaborate civil ceremonies. Modern experiments in alternatives to monogamous marriage, such as the communal living and free-love movements of the 1960s, quickly floundered, with most members going on to marry.[241] "There is universal cultural disapproval of casual sexual unions that create a child without a responsible father."[242] Evolutionary psychologists, it seems, arrive at the same conclusion:

> No community that practices unrestricted sexual relationships without anything resembling marriage has lasted for long. 'The new consensus,' noted feminist critic Ellen Willis, 'is that the family is our last refuge, our only defense against universal predatory selfishness, loneliness, and rootlessness.[243]

Selfishness. Loneliness. Rootlessness. These words seem a perfect reflection of the arc of *homo incurvatus in se*. (We put our own desires above all else, a path that leads through temporary pleasure to inevitable isolation, disconnectedness, and despair). They are also the antithesis of Augustine's divine view of the life God intended and His reason for creating "a companion" for Adam out of his own rib.

> God chose to make a single individual the starting point of all mankind . . . His purpose in this was that the human race should not merely be united in a society by natural likeness, but should also be

bound together by a kind of tie of kinship to form a harmonious unity, linked together by the "bond of Peace."[244]

Marriage, and having children within marriage, is the closest thing we have to recreating this "tie of kinship," but these ties are rapidly unfurling.

In 1960, 72% of all [American] adults ages 18 and older were married; today just 51% are. Other adult living arrangements—including cohabitation, single-person households and single parenthood—have all grown more prevalent in recent decades . . . Nearly four-in-ten Americans (39%) said they agree that marriage as an institution is becoming obsolete.[245]

Also,

Over the past 50 years, the share of children born to unmarried mothers has risen dramatically— increasing eightfold from 5% in 1960 to 41% in 2008 . . . 25% of American children age 14 or younger were living with only one parent in 2008.[246]

If sin has been with us since the Fall, it would stand to reason that disordered patterns of marriage and sexuality would be somewhat predictable. Why, then, should Americans in the 21st century be overly concerned about the current decline in marriage? "The scale of marital breakdowns in the West since 1960 has no historical precedent that I know of, and seems unique," notes retired Princeton University family historian, Lawrence Stone. "There has been nothing like it for the last 2000 years, and probably longer."[247] It is with no small urgency, then, that this thesis considers marriage, its decline, and the consequences to society. In the pages to follow, marriage will be considered in two respects: 1) freedom, and 2) responsibility. In each case, it will become clear that what was intended to be good and life-giving has been turned to "death" (Romans 6:23) by a few million individual acts of *homo incurvatus in se*.

freedom

Benjamin Franklin saw what America was up against from the very beginning: "Only a virtuous people are capable of freedom."[248] The American people in the early years of the "great experiment" were, unequivocally, virtuous. They "took for granted that marriage was the bedrock institution of society."[249] To them, virtue and morality were synonymous with "fidelity within marriage" and its ultimate permanence.[250] After returning from his extended American visit, Tocqueville observed that "morals are far more strict there than elsewhere."[251] Charles Murray parsed these "founding virtues" to four overarching themes: industriousness and honesty (which are virtues unto themselves, and will be touched on later), and marriage and religiosity,[252] "institutions through which right behavior is nurtured."[253] All who were involved in the creation of these United States understood that "its success depended on virtue in its citizenry."[254]

> 'To suppose that any form of government will secure liberty or happiness without any virtue in the people is a chimerical idea' (James Madison). It was chimerical because of the nearly unbridled freedom that the American Constitution allowed the citizens of the new nations. . . . Americans faced few legal restrictions on their freedom of action and no legal obligations to their neighbors except to refrain from harming them. The guides to their behavior at any more subtle level had to come from within.[255]

This "subtle level" of self-monitoring comes down, primarily, to this: how well we handle our freedom when it comes to sexual desire. This is hardly an American challenge. "The balance between sexual expression and restraint"[256] has been wrestled with across time and continents. The average American in the 1700s was no less susceptible to sexual temptation or marital dissatisfaction than the first man and woman or the people who took their vows this morning. These inner struggles are part of our fallen human nature, as first revealed in Genesis 3:7:

> The first discovery of our humanity, or better, the discovery that constitutes our humanity, is a discovery about our sexual being. . . . We

84

discover, first, our own permanent incompleteness. We have need for, and are dependent upon, a complementary yet different other, even to realize or satisfy our bodily nature. We learn that sex means that we are halves, not wholes, and worse, that we do not command the missing complementary half. . . . Neither are we internally whole. We are possessed by an unruly or rebellious 'autonomous' sexual nature within— one that does not heed our commands (any more than we heeded God's): we face also within an ungovernable and disobedient element, which embarrasses our claim to self-command.[257]

A deep-rooted appreciation for the notion of "complementary halves made whole" seems to be at the heart of the American ideal of marriage. Although women were a long way off from being equal partners under the law, they were, from the very beginning, given the right to choose their own husbands,[258] a departure from the arranged-marriage culture many had fled. Young American girls were then raised and educated so that they might be able to make such an important decision for themselves.[259] The fact that the founding fathers held this freedom of choice so dear reflected their view of the marriage bond as "a covenant."[260] Marriage, the founders believed, could only be sustained if the couple took their vows knowing they "were perfectly free not to have contracted them."[261] The early American admiration for the institution was best captured by James

Wilson in his *Letters on Law*:

> Whether we consult the soundest deductions of reason, or resort to the best information conveyed to us by history, or listen to the undoubted intelligence communicated in holy writ, we shall find, that to the institution of marriage the true origin of society must be traced. . . . To the institution, more than to any other, have mankind been indebted for the share of peace and harmony which has been distributed among them. "*Prima societas in ipso conjugio est,*" ("The first bond of society is marriage") says Cicero in his book of offices: a work which does honor to the human understanding and the human heart.[262]

What happened? How did the nation that started out holding marriage and virtue in such high regard fall so far? Well, for most of the American story, sexual consequences and social mores helped to temper urges to seek pleasure unbridled, and without obligation. This seemed to hold up through the 20th century. In the 1920s, there was a slight foreshadowing of rebellion against Victorian sexual codes and the resulting rise in premarital sex and divorce,[263] but by the 1950s, the pendulum had swung back. "Young people were not taught how to 'say no,' they were simply handed wedding rings."[264] Predictably, the age of first parenthood fell, fertility increased, and the divorce rate dipped from its post-war high.[265] Just as predictably, there was a counter rebellion, only this time there was a new weapon: the birth control pill. The consequences of sex—namely children—had never been easier to prevent, and no longer required the male's cooperation. As the consequences went, so too went the social mores—individual sin becoming collective sin and creating a social structure through which evil emanates. Parents who had had premarital sex in the 1960s, or fled stale marriages in the 70s, did not want to be hypocritical about sex when rearing their own children. By the 1990s, "4 out of 10 ninth graders—who but a few years ago were more patiently awaiting adulthood—reporting having had intercourse."[266]

What the "adults" call "recreational sex" the kids soon call "hook-ups," and the price they pay is anything but casual. "Increasing premarital sexual activity—more sex with more partners—has coincided with increases in sexually transmitted disease, rape, nonmarital pregnancy, cohabitation, and divorce."[267] Indulgence becomes habitual. Such is the one-way street that is *homo incurvatus in se*:

> It is not only a lack of a certain quality in the will, nor even only a lack of light in the mind or of power in the memory, but particularly it is a total lack of uprightness and of the power of all the faculties both of body and soul and of the whole inner and outer man. On top of all this, it is a propensity toward evil. It is a nausea toward the good, a loathing of light and wisdom, and a

delight in error and darkness, a flight from and an abomination of all good works, a pursuit of evil.[268]

And so America, the nation that once viewed marriage as the bedrock of its existence, continued down the slippery slope. Lacking the discipline to deny our desires, we no longer knew how to stick around "when the romance fades."[269] By the late 1960s, no-fault divorce made walking away not only easy but increasingly ordinary.[270] "Most marriages don't die of abuse or adultery. They die 'with a whimper, as people turn away from one another, slowly growing apart.'"[271] (Notice again the language of *turning away from the other*, and towards some unknown future where the sinful self is free to imagine there will never be boredom or annoyance or necessary effort). As the clear norm of marriage became murky, cohabitation became commonplace. By 1995, 58% of college students surveyed said they thought people should live together to "be sure they are compatible before marriage."[272] This despite the fact that there was already clear research showing the cohabitation increases the likelihood of divorce.[273]

People cohabit and sometimes divorce for the same reason—they just aren't that committed to marriage. Cohabitation is 'erotic timidity . . . at its core it is all about anxiety, commitment with fingers crossed.' It sees love as conditional rather than committed. If either partner becomes dissatisfied, he or she can seek bliss elsewhere.[274]

88

Again we see anxiety at the root of our ills. By removing the Judeo-Christian backdrop that supports the ideal of marriage in American culture, young people have only recent history to guide them—and recent history, as far as they can see, is nothing but a string of divorced parents, strangers in the master bedroom, and holidays spent being pulled in different directions. They are understandably anxious about marriage because they have so rarely seen it lived out, or lived out in a way that makes them believe that within that sacred bond there is something worth aspiring to—something greater than themselves. Living together feels like a risk-free trial, but when both parties enter with their fingers crossed, they are ill-equipped for the inevitable challenges of a mature relationship.

Even Augustine, who for many years "polluted the stream of friendship with my filthy desires,"[275] knew the difference between marriage and "shacking up."

> I lived with a girl not bound to me in lawful wedlock but sought out by the roving eye of reckless desire: all the same she was the only girl I had, and I was sexually faithful to her. This experience taught me first hand what a difference there is between a marriage contracted for the purpose of founding a family, and a relationship of love charged with carnal desire in which children may be born against the parent's wishes.[276]

We have said that the primary curbs that support and enforce marriage have historically been sexual consequences and social mores. It is not hard to imagine that as individuals became more inclined to reject sexual purity for themselves, they were less interested in condemning impurity in others. Shame, "the emotion that reveals a culture's moral norms,"[277] therefore, fell by the wayside in the final decades of the 20th century. Peer pressure—fueled by an overly sexual commercial and entertainment culture—was more inclined to promote than discourage sexual behavior. Sin, which now "fails to strike fear in the hearts of many religious believers," left the Church in the West straining "to find its bearings in a sexually charged landscape."[278] Christians could no longer claim to be an example, with a divorce rate equal to that of the general population.[279] And, as America entered the 21st century, the upper class—the group that is supposed to "set the standard for the society"[280]— seemed to have lost its sense of moral obligation. "The upper class still does a good job of practicing some of the virtues, but it no longer preaches them. It has lost self-confidence in the rightness of its own customs and values, and preaches nonjudgmentalism instead."[281] Although women with college degrees give birth out of wedlock less than 5%[282] of the time, it is "impermissible" in the new upper class to use "a derogatory label for nonmarital births."[283] In fact, successful, well-educated people today only consider it socially acceptable to pass judgment on three groups: "people with differing political views, fundamentalist Christians, and rural working-class whites."[284]

Without a culture that reinforces the virtues of marriage—and clearly articulates the relationship between marriage, education, and quality of life—the essential fabric of American democracy is eroded. How can there be trust, confidence, hope, justice, fellowship, independence, and love in a country in which only a minority are making good on the basic commitment to build a stable home. This seems the inevitable lesson of the gospel of Luke (16:10): "Whoever is faithful in a very little is faithful also in much." To trust in one's neighbors, to rely on a shared commitment to the greater good, to have faith that our children will be able to do the same, these great freedoms are founded on the presumption that every day, the vast majority of citizens are practicing being faithful to the small promises they made to their own families, such that they might have the skills of character needed to step up and assist with the larger needs of the community. Marriage, the essential tool of maturity and wisdom, has been sacrificed by our perpetual inward turn toward that one primal, disordered desire: freedom to be sexual without restraint.

> The physical and spatial metaphor of curvature . . . betrays a person withdrawn into a fixed, intense, self-regard, oblivious to her surroundings. The narrowness of such a gaze caused by its attention to only one object, causes us to miss the world (not to mention God) for what it is. All else sits in

the fuzziness of peripheral vision and is only seen in reference to the primary object, ourselves. The irony in the midst of our fixed focus on ourselves, however, is that our inattention to all that is not ourselves is part of the reason that we mis-read ourselves as well, not least in that we are 'lumpishly insensitive to the intensity of our predicament before God.'[285]

When America was a clean slate and our best and brightest were dedicated to creating a new nation that would support individual freedoms like no other before it, they understood full well that certain personal desires would need to be voluntarily renounced for the good of the whole. The price of those small denials was well worth the blessing of a nation that so wholeheartedly supported the rights of each man to reach his full potential. Somewhere along the line—most notably in the early 1960s—we allowed ourselves to forget the trade-off. Like kids at a birthday party who wanted nothing more than to lick the icing off the cupcakes, we began to value our sexual freedom above all else. Anyone who tried to point out the consequences of that trend was deemed "a square" and a "prig." The heart wants what the heart wants we declared—and now we have it, wretched consequences and all. By denying the timeless truth that "the first bond of society is marriage,"[286] and the corollary reality that, "as the bond goes, so goes society," *homo incurvatus in se* has put America's very future at risk.

92

responsibility

Despite our determination to separate pleasure from duty, it remains an inescapable fact of our anatomy: sex leads to babies and the responsibilities of child rearing. Just as sin has led us to make an end run around marriage, so, too, we have sought to avoid the responsibility intended to go hand in hand with sexual pleasure. Birth control—which is used by 62% of all U.S. woman of reproductive age[287]—and abortion are common options. Although it is encouraging to note that abortion rates in the U.S. are now at an historically low 18% of all pregnancies,[288] this still represents 227 aborted lives per every 1000 live births.[289] But, for the purposes of this brief section, the complex social and theological issues of birth control and abortion will not be addressed. Rather, responsibility will be considered as it pertains to those who have children, the impact that unmarried mothers are having on society, and the very problematic statistic that, increasingly, they are uneducated and white.[290] Much of this insight comes from the 2012 book, *Coming Apart: The State of White America, 1960-2010,* in which Charles Murray analyzes demographic data based not on the whole of the nation, but on its majority race.

> For decades now, trends in American life have been presented in terms of race and ethnicity, with non-Latino whites (hereafter, just whites) serving as the reference point—the black poverty rate compared to the white poverty rate, the

percentage of Latinos who go to college compared to the percentage of whites who go to college. . . . This strategy has distracted our attention from the way that the reference point is changing. . . . And so this book uses evidence based overwhelmingly on whites in . . . the new upper class [and] the new lower class. . . . My message: don't kid yourselves that we are looking at stresses that can be remedied by attacking the legacy of racism or by restricting immigration. The trends I describe exist independently of ethnic heritage.[291]

To synthesize and give narrative to the data, Murray comes us with two prototypical towns: Belmont, which represents the new upper-class—also know as "the cognitive elite"—in which 63% have BAs and the median family income in 2000 was $124,200, and Fishtown, which represents the growing lower class—a town in which some will finish high school, get GEDs, go to community college for a year or so, but most will work in both high and low-skill blue collar jobs, and only "8% of the adults" have college degrees.[292] We will use Murray's depictions of upscale Belmont and lower-class Fishtown to show how "over the last half century, marriage has become the fault line dividing American classes."[293] That fault line is leading with frightening speed to the "fracturing of human society" in America.

Trends in marriage are important not just with regard to the organization of communities, but because they are associated with large effects on the socialization of the next generation. No matter what the outcome being examined—the quality of mother-infant relationship, externalizing behavior in childhood (aggression, delinquency, and hyperactivity), delinquency in adolescence, criminality as adults, illness and injury in childhood, early mortality, sexual decision making in adolescence, school problems and dropping out, emotional health, or any other measure of how well or poorly children do in life—the family structure that produces the best outcomes for children, on average, are two biological parents who remain married. Divorced parents produce the next-best outcomes. Whether the parents remarry or remain single while the children are growing up makes little difference. Never-married women produce the worst outcomes.[294]

Tracing data as far back as the American Revolution, nonmarital births to white women held steady at well below 5% up through the 1960s.[295] "White children were conceived outside marriage at varying rates in different social classes, but hardly ever born outside marriage in any class."[296] Up through the 1960s, American marital norms had followed what Bronislaw Malinowski has referred to as a "universal sociological law."[297]

Every culture, he concluded, had a norm that 'no child should be brought into the world without a man—and one man at that—assuming the role of sociological father, that is, guardian and protector, the male link between the child and the rest of the community.' Without that man, 'the group consisting of a woman and her offspring is sociologically incomplete and illegitimate.'[298]

As cited earlier, "for the first time in human history,"[299] American society no longer considers a single, unmarried mother's children to be "illegitimate." With the stigma removed, one might think that white women across all classes—including the celebrated Murphy Brown-style successful single career women—would take advantage of this new "alternative," but they do not. The increases in nonmarital white births in America can be correlated almost entirely to education. With fewer than 16 years of education, it is more likely than not that a young woman will have a baby without a husband.[300] "For women who did not finish high school, the percentage was closing in on levels in excess of 60 percent of the live births that previously have been associated with the black underclass."[301] This was not always the case. In 1963, "the marriage percentages for college grads and highs school dropouts were about the same."[302] Marriage, in America, was never just for the chosen few. It was, as the founders intended, the bedrock of society—all of society.

Today, that society is breaking at both the local and national level, precipitated, to a large extent, by the dramatic rise in single, white mothers. Correlating three national longitudinal studies, Murray reveals this statistic about children whose mothers turned forty between 1997 and 2004: In Belmont, 90% still lived with both biological parents; in Fishtown, it was less than 30%. "The absolute level is so low that it calls into question the viability of white working-class communities as a place for socializing the next generation."[303] Some might argue that many of these unmarried women are, in fact, living with the biological father, or perhaps, another caring man so the children are just fine. The research does not support this claim.

> The disadvantages of being born to cohabiting parents extend into childhood and adolescence, even when the cohabiting couple stills consists of the two biological parents . . . the outcomes were rarely better than those for children living with a single parent or in a 'cohabiting stepparent' family.[304]

The reasons for this are myriad: married couples tend to become more religiously involved after marriage while cohabitating couples become less so, extended families support and invest in married couples and their children far more than they do for unmarried couples, schools and courts take far more seriously the role of legal father and husband than they do the sway of "mom's boyfriend."[305]

But perhaps the greatest reason is that "married partners tend to enhance their productivity by developing specialized skills; cohabiting partners more often do everything for themselves (being less sure of the partner's sticking around.) This helps account for the marriage premium—men's greater earning if married."[306]

Although many might not be aware of these specific statistics or the severity of them, America knows that there's a problem. An overwhelming majority (69%) of Americans say that "the trend toward more single women having children without a male partner to help raise them is a bad thing for society,"[307] and 61% that a child needs "both a mother and a father to grow up happily."[308] Those who insist that the disadvantages of being born into the lower class are just too great to overcome may not be aware that the odds of building a better future are—even now—very much on their side. They simply have to make good on three highly manageable goals: 1) graduate from high school, 2) get a job, and 3) get married and wait until they're 21 before having a baby.[309] If they manage that, according to Brookings economists Ron Haskins and Isabel Sawhill, "they have an almost 75% chance of making it into the middle class."[310] Still, few are willing or able to reassert the obvious: that having kids outside of marriage is bad for the kids, bad for parents, and bad for the community. "Today, to suggest that a change might be in order, starting with a healthy drop in self-absorption, is anathema: it's a free country, and don't lay your values on my self-respect."[311]

So where are the men in all this? Their increasingly marginalized role may be the most dangerous thing to American society of all. Again, we must look at education, and the role it plays in both marriage and responsibility. We will also consider one of Murray's founding virtues—industriousness—as it pertains to the men of Fishtown. One of the great virtues of America is that it did not have "different codes for socioeconomic classes."[312] Young men of all backgrounds were raised in the Judeo-Christian codes of conduct exemplified in the classic McGuffey Readers, which taught America's children who and what they were and how they were expected to behave.[313] Even when these civic training guides were phased out, their lessons endured, so that a man growing up in the 1940s, 50s, and even early 60s, could be expected to hold this view of the code for males:

> To be a man means that you are brave, loyal, and true. When you are in the wrong, you own up and take your punishment. You don't take advantage of women. As a husband, you support and protect your wife and children. You are gracious in victory and a good sport in defeat. Your word is you bond. Your handshake is as good as your word. It's not whether you win or lose, but how you play the game. When the ship goes down, you

put the women and children into the lifeboats and wave good-bye with a smile.[314]

Up through the 1980s, changes in Fishtown's "male dropout from the labor force moved roughly in tandem with the national unemployment rate."[315] But between 1985 and 2005, something changed:

> Men who had not completed high school increased their leisure time by eight hours per week, while men who had completed college decreased their leisure time by six hours per week. In 2003-5, men who were not employed spent less time on job search, education, and training, and doing useful things around the house than they had in 1985. They spent less time on civic and religious activities. They didn't even spend their leisure time on active pastimes such as exercise, sports, hobbies, or reading ... How did they spend that extra leisure time? Sleeping and watching television.[316]

This sleeping and TV watching is, no doubt, related to an increase in drug and alcohol use. "With the economy—the factories all gone—and the poverty, you can get sucked into drugs real easy."[317] Entertainment imitates life. In the past five years, movies such as *Ted, The 40-Year Old Virgin, Knocked Up,* and *Pineapple Express* depict the new prototypical American male: hanging out on the couch with his buddies well into his 30s, playing video games, dodging serious relationships, and getting stoned. This makes women—often the mothers of their children—less inclined to want them as spouses, which, in turn, may keep them from maturing. *Homo incurvatus in se* is a vicious cycle. "Married men become more productive after they are married *because* they are married."[318] Men who marry are also less likely to suffer from depression, and those who do suffer in their bachelorhood will find that marriage "mitigates against moroseness."[319] In his book *Sexual Suicide*, George Gilder claimed that "unmarried males arriving at adulthood are barbarians who are then civilized by women through marriage."[320] He predicted that because of this, the decline in marriage in America would be disastrous. Many derided his claim as "patriarchal sexism," but Murray contends that its underlying assertions ring true: "The responsibilities of marriage induce young men to settle down, focus, and get to work."[321] In Murray's 21st-century Fishtown, over 30% of white males ages 30-49 are considered economically ineffectual. In other words, even by the lowest measure—keeping themselves and one other adult above the poverty line—they are failing.[322]

This failure is felt and shared by not only the people of Fishtown, but by all of America who will wrestle with how to keep the unemployed afloat, how to absorb the increase in mental illness, violence, drug abuse, and crime that is triggered by this new generation of ineffectual men and overburdened women, and how to sustain the promise of "equality" in America when circumstances have grown so far from equal. There had been a time when young men and women of all social classes would be overwhelmed with desire and yield. If a child were conceived, the next step was clear—or if it were not, society would make it clear. Once we realized how easy it could be to have pleasure without responsibility, our sinful natures had a field day, heaping lie upon lie (you don't need a man to have a baby, a marriage license is just a piece of paper, marriage is old-fashioned, the kids are just fine), until we fall victim to what Luther noted five-hundred years ago:

> Curvedness is now natural for us, a natural wickedness and a natural sinfulness. Thus man has no help from his natural powers, but he needs the aid of some power outside of himself. This is love.[323]

The love of which Luther speaks can only be found in God. So although we don't need God to make a case for the importance of marriage to society, we cannot be saved from the sin that has led to its decline without Him. The one who created us, redeems us, and sanctifies us is our only hope against *homo incurvatus in se* and the resurrection of the institution of marriage.

vocation

Vocation, from the Latin *vocatio*, can mean several things: "the proclamation of the gospel, through which human beings are called to be children of God,"[324] the call to the divine office of teaching and preaching,[325] and the work each one of us is called to do in our daily lives.[326] Luther emphasizes this third use, underscored by the passage from 1 Corinthians 7:20 that says, "each shall remain in the same vocation (*klesis*) in which he was called."[327] It is this understanding of vocation that will be the focus of this section.

Luther, and many others, view vocation as the way God "has chosen to work through human beings, who in their different capacities and according to their different talents, serve each other."[328] We serve each other as husband and wife, as mother and father, and neighbor and friend. We serve each other through our talents and professions, the fruits of our labors meeting the needs of others. Luther interprets Christ's command against being anxious through the lens of vocation, expanding on the "trust" of the lilies and the birds:

> 'He gives the wool, but not without our labor. If it is on the sheep, it makes no garment.' God gives the wool, but it must be sheared, carded, spun, etc. In these vocations God's creative work moves on, coming to its destination only with the neighbor who needs the clothing.[329]

And so we see that trust in God and trust in neighbor—as well as reliance on God and on neighbor to use their talents rightly—are essential to the great economy of vocation. "Whether we want to accept it or not, self-sufficiency is an illusion. We do depend on other people—the farmer, the plumber who puts in our water system, the doctor, our parents—for our very lives."[330] As we have turned away from God, we have turned away from the gift of vocation, which orients us in particular relations to others and their needs. We have thrown ourselves into work that was not intended for us in pursuit of greater wealth and power. We have grown bitter about daily tasks because we have forgotten that God is working through them. We have lost our trust in our fellow man, who is as self-absorbed as we are. This social trust—not just "trust in a particular neighbor who happens to be your friend, but a generalized expectation that the people around you will do the right thing"[331]—is the raw material that makes community possible. In America's Fishtowns, social trust has been so greatly diminished that it may well be irreparable.[332] And although America's upscale Belmonts do have a higher degree of trust, it is only within their own sphere: since interaction between the upper and lower classes is rapidly decreasing, so, too, is trust. This disrupts vocation's ability to make good on the promise that "from everyone who has been given much, much will be demanded" (Luke 12:48). This may well be what the wealthy are afraid of—that the blessings of a mixed community all move in one direction. This fear ignores the fact that the financially well-off will, in their lifetime, be just as likely to suffer illness, brokenness, abandonment, helplessness, or loss of stature or purpose, and that wisdom in these areas are just as likely to come from a plumber as a fellow investment broker.

When we are in right relation to God and neighbor, and we have a proper understanding of vocation, we can see that our callings change throughout our lives:

> A young man working his way through college may get a job in a fast-food restaurant. For the time being, that's his vocation, and he is to love and serve his customers and his shift manager by flipping hamburgers. If he is fortunate enough to be going to college, he also has the vocation of being a student, which has specific obligations of its own (study!). Eventually he may get that computer degree, and he may go into his lifework. That will be his vocation then. And if his dot.com company goes bankrupt, and he goes from vast wealth back to flipping burgers, he has a new vocation. At every stage his calling is not something that will wait until he graduates, or even until he gets that big promotion. Vocation is in the here and now.[333]

In contrast, a secular notion of "vocation" as some ultimate level of success and comfort that we aspire to earn and keep, and to which we are entitled—as well as the skewed view of manual labor as a lesser call—has exacerbated our disordered view of work in the scope of our daily lives. Timothy Keller, author of *Every Good*

Endeavor, offers new insight into our current American predicament. Surveying the United States' privileged "knowledge classes," Dr. Keller describes

> a population that is "work obsessed," holding their jobs to be the fount of "self-fulfillment and self-realization," seeing leisure as merely "work stoppage for bodily repair" and allowing office principles like "efficiency, value and speed" to infuse and overwhelm their personal lives. In this world, where work becomes the chief source of identity and meaning, families ache and—from Wall Street to elite sports to political office—dishonesty abounds, because professional loss can sink a person's sense of being. . . . At the other end of the class spectrum [is an] equal and opposite pathology: a common perception of work as miserable toil, inherently 'frustrating and exhausting,' to be 'avoided or simply endured ... Keller argues for a centrist understanding of work as calling—work that lends life meaning but doesn't monopolize it, work that is performed not for personal glory but in service of others. He challenges the idea . . . that 'work is a curse and that something else (leisure, family, or even 'spiritual' pursuits) is the only way to find meaning in life'; and he criticizes 'the opposite mistake, namely, that work is the only important human activity and that rest is a necessary evil—

something we do strictly to 'recharge our batteries' in order to continue to work.[334]

Even those without religious faith or an informed view on vocation would recognize the truth in Dr. Keller's words. But taking action on them is something else entirely. For this people need God. Without a worldview of life as blessing, in which "darkness and light are all the same" (Psalm 139:12) and one lives and breathes in full confidence that salvation has already been secured—and there is nothing left of value to earn—there is no way to understand that flipping burgers and running a successful dot.com are equal endeavors. Even with a Christian worldview, it is hard for Americans to shake their "return on investment" mentality. Our ever-anxious selves continue to assert that every ounce of effort must pay rich dividends in a determined ascent to the top—some fictional heaven where one's social standing and financial security seem sufficient to cushion one from earthly suffering. They, too, it seems, forget that God's notion of "return on investment" for each one of our lives was spelled out in Isaiah 55:10:

> For as the rain and the snow come down from heaven, and do not return there until they have watered the earth, making it bring forth and sprout, giving see to the sower and bread to the eater, so shall my word be that goes out from my mouth; it shall not return to me empty, but shall accomplish

that which I purpose, and succeed in the thing for which I sent it.

So how does our sinful oblivion to God's purposes for us through the blessing of *vocatio* lead to the "fracturing of human society"[335] in 21st-century America? We consider this now briefly in two aspects: 1) proximity and 2) participation.

proximity

One hundred years after the founding of the nation, Alexis de Tocqueville opined that the heart of the despot is egotism. "A despot easily forgives his subjects for not loving him, provided they do not love each other."[336] This, he asserted, could never happen in the United States because

> Local freedom . . . perpetually brings men together, and forces them to help one another, in spite of the propensities which sever them. In the United States, the more opulent citizens take great care not to stand aloof from the people. On the contrary, they constantly keep on easy terms with the lower classes: they listen to them, they speak to them every day.[337]

For the first time in America's history, this easy and constant contact between the upper and lower classes is no longer the norm. The chasm is prompted by the upper class whose wealth and education has grown dramatically: in the 1960s, only 8% of Americans had incomes over $100,000 (in 2010 dollars) with the top centile at $200,000 or more.[338] Moving into the 1980s, the bottom quartile of Americans fell, the middle went flat, and the upper centiles exploded such that by 2009, the *lowest* salary in the top 1% was $441,000.[339] This gain in income earnings was fueled to a great degree by elite educations and marriages born within those select communities. This would seem to be a blessing to society and, had these cognitively superior, highly educated, newly-affluent couples chosen to live and work within the larger society, this might well have been true. But the new "cognitive elite" are not like the upper class and the power brokers of the past.

> As of 1960, the people who had risen to the top had little in common except their success. . . . The world in which David Rockefeller . . . grew up could not have been more different from the world of the Jewish immigrants and sons of immigrant who built Hollywood and pioneered radio and television broadcasting. . . . The men who were the leaders at CBS News in 1960 included the son of a farmer, . . . the son of a Kansas City dentist who dropped out of college to become a newspaper reporter, and a Rhodes scholar. . . . The Kennedy administration . . . consisted of three sons of small farmers, and the sons of a sales manager of a shoe company, the

owner of a struggling menswear store, and immigrant factory worker, and an immigrant who made his living peddling produce.[340]

Today's "narrow elite" are, by contrast, increasingly homogamous (created by parents of similar education and/or cognitive ability).[341] College graduates are tending to marry other college graduates.[342] Their children are born with higher IQs than the average, and with the benefits of private school education, extracurricular opportunities, tutoring, and test preparation, all of which increase their odds of getting into an elite university. In the 1990s, for example, 79% of "Tier-1" college students came from the top quartile of socioeconomic status. Only 2% came from the bottom 25%.[343] So the promise of education as the great equalizer no longer holds true for most. Marriage is also quickly losing its ability to create the "ties of kinship" across socioeconomic lines. As the Ivy Leagues and other Tier-1 colleges have become cognitive "sorting machines,"[344] the entire make-up of those student bodies has changed such that a student who tests in the top 5% on the SAT or ACT may go through their entire collegiate socialization period without interacting with anyone who is not equally gifted.[345] These intellectually superior young people develop their own cultural tastes, norms, and identifiers, which may well include a lack of empathy for anyone with less ability or opportunity. As a result, by the end of the 20th century, when they began their careers and their married lives, "the well educated and the affluent increasingly segmented themselves off from the rest of American society."[346] Their ultimate destination? The "Superzips," zip code areas in which the combination of education and income places a resident in the 95-99 percentile of all Americans.[347]

In this self-selected retreat from "the rabble,"[348] we can see an entire class of people "turned in on themselves." God-given intelligence is hardly a sin—it is a good gift with a right use according to vocation—but intelligence alone has not created this new separatism. In the early part of the 20th century, the average state college in Pennsylvania had as many high-IQ students as Harvard or Yale.[349] Even through the 1950s, "elite colleges did not have exceptionally talented student bodies."[350] Then, for a variety of reasons, the 1960s ushered in the era of widespread SAT taking. Much of the push was led by academic pioneers who hoped to discover America's best and brightest, groom them in the best universities, and channel those abilities for the common good.[351] It was idealism at its best, and could have been a useful instrument in the purposes of divine vocation, but America's best and brightest weren't, it seemed, particularly interested in the serving others, opting instead for careers as "well-paid, securely positioned providers[s] of expert advice: corporate lawyer, investment banker, management consultant, high-end specialized doctor."[352] Within a few short generations, the spirit of "ask not what your country can do for you" had evaporated, with the new elite feeling increasingly entitled to create a lifestyle "in their own image." They would pay taxes and support charities, but their children would not got to school, or church, or play sports, or have sleepovers with anyone whose parents had not come up through the same ivied ranks, leaving the new upper class "balkanized."[353]

> Their ignorance about other Americans is more problematic than the ignorance of other Americans about them. It is not a problem if a truck driver cannot empathize with the priorities of Yale professors. It is a problem if Yale professors, or producers of network news programs, or CEOs of great corporations, or presidential advisors cannot empathize with the priorities of truck drivers.[354]

Luther reminds us that "the Spirit of God can arise only when the pride of the flesh has been humbled."[355] In America's new elites, we see how the sin of pride has led an entire class to turn away from God and neighbor.

Not surprisingly, the upper class is not the only group guilty of wanting to be separated by net worth. Robert Reich calls this phenomenon the 'secession of the successful,'[356] and we can see it all across America in our love for the gated and planned communities that have created the new suburban sprawl. "Today's suburban reality finds its origins in the pastoral dream of the autonomous homestead in the countryside, [but] as the middle class rushes to build its countryside cottages at the same time on the same land, the resulting environment is inevitably unsatisfying, its objective self-contradictory: isolation en masse."[357] More disturbing is how these subdivisions are broken in "clusters" that are distinguished by increments of buying power.

> Our history is fraught with many different types of segregation—by race, by class, by how recently one has immigrated—but for the first time we are now experiencing ruthless segregation by minute gradations of income. There have always been better and worse neighborhoods, and the rich have often taken refuge from the poor, but never with such precision. It would appear that, for many, there is little distinction between someone slightly less wealthy than themselves and a Skid Row bum.[358]

In many ways, the new development style has left homebuyers little choice but to abandon any sense of belonging to a socioeconomically diverse community. So powerful is the lure of the home with the white picket fence—or rather, the home with the great room, the walk-in closets, and the Jacuzzi tub—that anxiety overrides our deepest human needs. As families grow, or wealth increases, this extreme segmentation forces them to relocate to a more upscale "cluster."[359] This undermines one of the fundamental desires of the American Dream, to be a part of a community. "The traditional neighborhood—represented by mixed use, pedestrian-friendly communities of varied population"[360] has been replaced in America by sprawl. This sprawl is defined by clusters of pre-fab homes with nearby shopping centers and office parks connected by roadways.[361] This design all but eliminates pedestrian traffic, one of the activities that make a person feel connected to a community. "In suburbia, there is only one available lifestyle: to own a car and to need it for everything."[362]

And so, from the privacy of our own vehicles, we disappear behind our automated garage doors—harried from traffic created by plans that force everyone down single feeder roads[363]— into our spacious "cookie-cutter" homes. We are unaware that these new "communities" were not conceived with either individual happiness or the common good in mind, but with the single goal of maximizing profits for the developers of the homes and shopping malls and office parks, the sin of corporate greed now defining the daily lives of the majority of new American homeowners. The homeowners, meanwhile, had been guilty of the sin of pride, wanting a home that enhanced their sense of "having arrived," as well as the ability to be unharrassed by "others" when they get there—the ultimate extrinsic reward. Together these sins of turning inward and away from the needs of others has created, predictably, a scenario where "eight out of every ten new homes is gated"[364]and the likelihood of our "coming together voluntarily to solve our joint problems,"[365] as our Founding Fathers envisioned, is increasingly ancient history. Such is the fruit of *homo incurvatus in se*, which has severed our ties to *vocatio* through how and where we choose to live.

participation

Participation in the larger society gives individuals a sense of shared purpose and belonging. It is the glue that binds a community. It serves the common good as well as the individual, buffering souls—who will forever be tempted to turn inward—by drawing them out of themselves. Participation is one of the blessings of vocation and has always been one of the defining characteristics of American life. Again, we consider Tocqueville's views in our nation's early years:

> There are not only commercial and industrial associations in which all take part, but others of a thousand different types—religious, moral, serious, futile, very general and very limited, immensely large and very minute. Americans combine to give fetes, found seminaries, build churches, distribute books, and send missionaries to the antipodes. Hospitals, prisons, and schools take place in that way. Finally, if they want to proclaim a truth or propagate some feeling by the encouragement of a great example, they form an association.[366]

This level of civic participation is described by social scientists, including *Bowling Alone* author Robert Putnam, as *social capital*, a combination of neighborliness and civic engagement that benefits both the individual and the group. The title for his book came from the realization that as America reached the 21st century, bowling had grown in popularity while participation in bowling leagues had dropped by 73%.[367] This would hardly be cause for alarm if it weren't indicative of a much wider trend towards civic disengagement. Comparing statistics from the mid-1970s to the mid-1990s—and focusing on the cohort of 18-29 year olds (who would be in their mid-30s to 40s in 2012)—we see a pattern: read newspaper daily, down 57%; attended church weekly, down 30%; signed a petition, down 46%; attended public meeting, down 57%; officer or committee member of local organization, down 53%; union member, down 64%.[368] Tom Kissel, the national membership director for VFW Post 2378 in Berwyn, Illinois, a long time "'home away from home' for local veterans and a kind of working-class country club for the neighborhood,"[369] has seen membership dwindle so far they can hardly pay taxes on the building. "Kids today just aren't joiners."[370] Secular fraternal organizations such as the VFW—or the Elks, Moose, or Odd Fellows Clubs—were once "a central feature of American civic life."[371] Unlike today, where they are mostly unknown, or disregarded as lower-middle class men's clubs,[372] these groups once "drew their membership from across the social classes, and ensured regular, close interaction among people of different classes."[373] In Theda Skocpol's 2003 book, *Diminished Democracy*, she observed:

Read biographical sketches of prominent men and women of the past . . . and you will see proudly proclaimed memberships and officer-ships in a wide array of the same fraternal, veterans', women's, and civic associations that also involved millions of non-elite citizens. . . . Those who were leaders had to care about inspiring large numbers of fellow members. Members counted; and leaders had to mobilize and interact with others from a wide range of backgrounds or they were not successful.[374]

So civic engagement is not only about getting things done and solving our joint problems but in forming relationships, binding us together, and strengthening social trust as citizens of a shared democracy. Voting, one of the great privileges of a democracy, reveals the same pattern of growing apathy. Whereas adults in the first half of the 20th century voted at a rate upward of 80%,[375] today's Millennials participate at half that rate.[376] Despite their interest in a handful of social issues, and the high, under-30 turnout (51%) for Barack Obama in 2008, millennial participation in the presidential election was forecast to drop to 34% in 2012. And although Millennials now make up 25% of all eligible voters, their registration levels leading up to 2012 were the lowest in the last five presidential elections.[377] This may not be surprising given that this young cohort is comprised of the offspring of the Baby Boomers who, despite a burst of social activism in the early college years, are "less likely to be interested in politics, less likely to follow politics with any regularity, less likely to express a political opinion, and less likely to have accurate information relevant to politics."[378] Expanding on the Boomer zeitgeist, Putnam observes,

> It is a generation which, relative to earlier generations, rejects the norms and institutions that are central to the political system of which they are a part. What distinguishes this generation most is what it *does not like* or *does not do*, and not what it likes or does.[379]

We can see in this phrasing the footprint of *homo incurvatus in se*. A turning away rather than a turning towards. A rejection rather than an embrace. And although the figures tell a national story of increased apathy, the whole story cannot be told without considering, once again, the dividing line of income and education. Because in the new upper class, civic life is, actually, alive and well. People raise money, attend meetings, support school and social issues, join professional and neighborhood clubs, and display civic pride in their own select enclaves.[380] The new forms of social capital made available through the internet and social networking—hoped to be a democratizer—is enjoyed nearly twice as often by those with incomes over $75,000 than by those who make less than $30,000. Not surprisingly, participation in most working class cities and towns has dropped precipitously. In many ways, the people of American's Fishtowns no longer have the "luxury" of recognizing that vocation includes many roles, including "member of a community." Trapped in cycles of anxiety, depression, joblessness, and addiction, they can hardly conceive of any purpose for their lives greater than getting through the day. In Murray's Fishtown, social disengagement rose from an already high 63% in the 1970s to 75% in 2004, while civic disengagement went from 69% to a stunning 82% in that same period.

> The role of marriage—specifically, marriage with children—is obvious. Some large proportion of the webs of engagement in an ordinary community are spun because of the environment that parents are trying to foster for their children—through the schools, but also in everything from getting a new swing set for the park to prompting city council to install four-way stop signs on an intersection where children play. Married fathers are a good source of labor for these tasks. Unmarried fathers are not. . . . Meanwhile, single mothers who want to foster the right environment for their children are usually doing double duty, trying to be the breadwinner and an attentive parent at the same time. Few single mothers have much time or energy to spare for community activities.[381]

In the beginning of Chapter 2, we looked at the American pursuit of happiness. As we close out Chapter

3, it is worth noting that when the founding virtues—
honesty, industriousness, marriage, religiosity—are all in
place, the people in Fishtown and Belmont are about
equal in terms of happiness.[382] In other words, "there is
no inherent barrier to happiness for the person with a low
level of education holding a low-skill job."[383] The sorts of
activities which boost a person's level of happiness are
volunteering, attending club meetings, attending church,
and entertaining at home,[384] all things which can—and
traditionally have been—enjoyed by Americans of all
classes and income levels. In the past 50 years, "roughly
half the decline in contentment is associated with
financial worries, and half is associated with decline in
social capital: lower marriage rates and decreasing
connectedness to friends and community."[385]

In other words, we have ceased to trust in God's
promise to provide for us, and ceased to act on his call to
serve the common good with our God-given abilities.
Overwhelmed and consumed with worry, we turn ever
inward, compounding the culture of "every man for
himself" that we helped to create. This rejection, the
primal "turning away" from God that is *homo incurvatus
in se*, leads secular experts to describe the same result,
minus the language of "sin." Psychologist Martin
Seligman argues that

> more of us are feeling down because modern
> society encourages a belief in personal control
> and autonomy more than a commitment to duty

and common enterprise. This transformation
heightens our expectations about what we can
achieve through choice and grit and leaves us
unprepared to deal with life's inevitable failures.
Where once we could fall back on social capital—
families, churches, friends—these no longer are
strong enough to cushion our fall. In our personal
lives as well as in our collective life, the evidence . . .
suggests we are paying a significant price for a
quarter century's disengagement from one another.[386]

From almost any vantage point, the truth of our sin can be
seen. But without a theological understanding of sin,
there is no help for our suffering. It is up, then, to the
Church and its Body to connect the dots of our bleak
cultural reality to the saving grace of the Gospel. If one
can begin to see that she is, in fact, "turned in on herself,"
and that this has led only to greater suffering for herself
and others, there may be an opening for the message of
repentance. Perhaps we are finally broken enough to
listen. To turn back to God and to neighbor. Perhaps,
united in brokenness, we can rebuild the "ties of kinship"
that once upheld the American ideal. The findings of this
thesis, however challenging, do point to hope because
"eventually the myth of self-sufficiency sours, and we are
left staring at our neediness, confronted with the
brokenness and pain that have shadowed independence
throughout human history . . . but the gift of pain draws
us into community with God and one another."[387]

chapter 4

man turned in as a
way in to the gospel

In the beginning, God didn't make just two people: he made a bunch of us. Because he wanted us to have a lot of fun, and you can't really have fun unless there's a whole gang of you. He put us in Eden which was a combination garden and playground and park and told us to have fun.

At first we did have fun just like he expected. We rolled down the hills, waded in the streams, climbed on the trees, swung on the vines, ran in the meadows, frolicked in the woods, hid in the forest, and acted silly. We laughed a lot.

Then one day this snake told us that we weren't having real fun because we weren't keeping score. Back then, we didn't know what score was. When he explained it, we still couldn't see the fun. But he said we should give an apple to the person who was best at all the games and we'd never know who was best without keeping score. We could all see the fun of that, of course, because were were all sure we were the best.

It was different after that. We yelled a lot. We had to make up new scoring rules for most of the games. Others, like frolicking, we stopped playing because they were too hard to score.

By the time God found out what had happened we were spending about 45 minutes a day actually playing and the rest of the time working out scoring. God was wroth about that—— very, very wroth. He said we couldn't use his garden anymore because we weren't having fun. We told him we were having lots of fun. He was just being narrow minded because it wasn't exactly the kind of fun he originally thought of.

He wouldn't listen.

He kicked us out, and he said we couldn't come back until we stopped keeping score. To rub it in (to get our attention, he said), he told us we were all going to die and our scores wouldn't mean anything anyway.

He was wrong. My cumulative, all-game score now is 16,548 and that means a lot to me. If I can raise it to 20,000 before I die, I'll know I've accomplished something. Even if I can't my life has a great deal of meaning because I've taught my children to score high and they'll be able to reach 20,000 or even 30,000.

Really, it was life in the garden that didn't mean anything. Fun is great in its place but without scoring there's no reason for it. God actually has a very superficial view of life and I'm certainly glad my children are being raised away from his influence. We were lucky. We're all very grateful to the snake.
—Anne Herbert[388]

In the study of Biblical Theology, one learns the power of metaphor to communicate the Gospel message. This allows the uninitiated to understand a new concept in relationship to a familiar one. In the same way, poetry, prose, films, music, fiction, and conversations that allow for an opening—without hammering the nails in the cross before every Amen—help make a new concept understandable to the nonbeliever. In the "retelling" of the Creation narrative by Anne Herbert, the truths of our modern predicament shine through. It makes clear the symptoms and the culprit. It allows the Christian outsider to gain a toehold in the conversation about our sinful natures, how we came to be that way, and how we are paying the price for it now. It reveals how *homo incurvatus in se* has turned us into the wretched "score-keepers" that we are today. It begins a conversation.

If the goal of the Great Commission is to reach people with the Gospel message then—in the spirit of Pentecost—we must be fearless in crafting messages in such a way that it can be heard. This is not a matter of watering down doctrine, or preaching Glory over the Cross. It is a matter of recognizing that with no effective support from the culture, the 21st-century American church must first reeducate the seeking soul about this inescapable fact:

> From the moment a creature becomes aware of God as God and of itself as self, the terrible alternative of choosing God or self for the centre

> is opened to it. . . . Thus all day long, all the days
> of our life, we are sliding, slipping, falling
> away—as if God were, to our present
> consciousness, a smooth inclined plane on which
> there is no resting.[389]

Those who seek to lead people to the "easy yoke" of
Jesus must remember that the path to understanding may
require many different "inroads" to the truth, and a
productive series of "openings" that allows those baby
steps to progress without too many jarring obstacles. This
requires us to reclaim the meaning of *preaching* in the
Greek *khrvssw* (kerusso)[390] as heralding the 'good tidings
of God' to the non-Christian world.[391] With this audience
as our primary concern, we will be mindful that the
Gospel presented as "Jesus died on the cross for our sins"
may simply compress more into a single message than
one so far removed from an inkling of sin—and
predisposed to think negatively about Jesus based on the
unappealing behavior of many Christians—is able to take
in. If Christianity is now faced with having to "preach the
diagnosis"[392] before it can reveal "the cure," then we
must be willing to begin the conversation outside the
talking point script of doctrine.

The audience is more primed than we might
believe. In 1993, First Lady Hillary Rodham Clinton gave
a speech that addressed the American "sleeping sickness
of the soul."[393]

We enjoy economic growth, yet paradoxically 'we lack at some core level meaning in our individual lives and meaning collectively, that sense that our lives are part of some greater effort, that we are connected to one another, that community means that we have a place where we belong no matter who we are.' Underneath the 'hopeless girls with babies and angry boys with guns,' underneath the breakdown of civility and community, underneath the alienation that marks our 'acquisitive and competitive corporate culture' is, she said, spiritual poverty.[394]

This same message has been heard from any number of surprising sources:

"The real problem of *modernity* is the problem of belief," observed sociologist Daniel Bell. "To use an unfashionable term, it is a spiritual crisis."[395] Norman Lear, television producer and founder of the progressive liberal advocacy group People for the American Way, claimed that, "At no time in my life has our culture been so estranged from spiritual values. . . . Our problems are not economic and political. They are moral and spiritual—and must be addressed on that level if real solutions are to be found."[396] *New York Times* columnist and popular non-fiction writer Anna Quindlen explains the problems this way:

There is a yawning hole in the psyche of America and Americans where our sense of common purpose, of community and connection, of hope and a spiritual satisfaction should be. . . . We liberals must acknowledge this: that while the rights of the individual are precious, at some deep level individualism alone does not suffice. And the ability of the radical right to seize and exploit the terrain of the soul has been helped immeasurably by the failure of so many of the rest of us to even acknowledge the soul's existence.[397]

The focus on "liberal" writers and thinkers here is intentional. In a thesis grounded on the truths of Augustine and Luther, we see that the consequences of *homo incurvatus in se* belong to everyone. In sin we are united. In sin we are all equal, from Belmont to Fishtown and every cul-de-sac in between. "For there is no distinction, since all have sinned and fall short of the glory of God" (Romans 3: 22b-23). In a world that is clamoring to "level the playing field," here is the one way in which we always have and always will be "the same." If we are able to recognize this truth, we might also begin to unite on the one path to salvation that the Creator has given us—a path in which "there is no longer Jew or Greek, there is no longer slave or free, there is no longer male and female; for all of you are one in Christ Jesus" (Galatians 3:28).

The cacophonous movements that align social issues with political parties in the name of Christianity have, unfortunately, put profound barriers in the way of Grace. The name of Jesus Christ has been badly sullied by those who seek to make Him the spokesperson for this issue or that. Equally problematic, the radical shift in the distribution of wealth has made it harder for the 1% to feel the full weight of the human predicament, and for the lower classes to put aside their shame and despair long enough to put themselves within earshot of hope. The Church, then, must step up, finding its voice not by soft-pedaling the message, but by helping a God-starved culture find its way home. Where, in the past few decades, many churches have attempted to do this by "skipping over" the message of sin and heavying up on the "Jesus talk," this thesis recommends the reverse: begin with sin, or rather, the symptoms and consequences of sin. Using the image of *homo incurvatus in se* as your guide, unveil our shared and fallen reality in steps, allowing the spiritually superficial American culture to recognize first their broken nature, then the voice of their Creator, and finally, the awesome grace of a loving savior. Law and Gospel, yes, but not all in one bite.

As our common cries attest, the soil is loosed. Americans speak of the "spiritual" more comfortably. They are aware that the culture is not right somehow. Although the word "Jesus" has never been more divisive, one can say "God" at a cocktail party without scorn.

God has made a comeback, and with him, inevitably, sin. For you can't have one without the other. God looks a little different in each century, and sin does, too. Through one, we can effectively get to know the other.[398]

Everything old is new again. Consider how medieval Gregorian Chant, group chorales of Handel's Messiah, and *Kaballah*, an ancient Jewish sect, suddenly became all the rage in the late 20th century. *Homo incurvatus in se*, with its ancient Latin whiff of "authenticity" has the potential to be seen as fresh—even hip. Bolster that with the considerable weight of this historic but forgotten fact: "sin" has been an accepted fact of our humanity in every recorded culture.

The modern view that "sin" is some "guilt trip" that Jesus whipped up can be put aside with easily verifiable evidence: by the time Jesus came around, sin was old news. It was, in fact, the reason his message of repentance and grace was meaningful. By separating sin from Jesus at the *beginning* of a conversation, one might stand a better chance of leading a nonbeliever to *the end*, where sin and Christ will be united forever in the atonement.

So begin with this: the idea that man is turned in on himself and that this is the cause of much of his suffering. Refer to some of the physical images captured in Chapter 1:

Picture a body curved inward—in the fetal position, for example. The shape of the curve does two things: 1) it protects and defends the thing it is turned in on, guarding it and the right to have it to oneself, preferably in the secret shadow of the curve, and 2) its curved form creates a barrier between the heart's desire and the things it wants to keep at bay: judgment, change, help, love, God. When man is turned in on his own desires, the world—despite man's best efforts to the contrary— becomes smaller and darker. Without the impetus or wherewithal to reverse his course, his condition gets progressively worse. Without access to any power greater than himself—and with the sudden realization that he is, in fact, only human—he becomes trapped in the "hamster wheel" of his own thoughts and enslaved by his own feelings and desires.

Use your hands. Demonstrate a body turned in on itself with a downward facing clenched fist. Discuss whether or not this is a state likely to lead to health, light, and life. Unclench it slightly. Show where there is now room for light, help, grace to enter. Make your palm flat and begin to tilt it upward. Show how this might be what our souls look like as they become willing to yield to help, to God, to the life that we were born for. *Sursum cor!* Now, turn the palm all the way around and outward. Consider if perhaps the person "turned out towards others" is not in a more likely state to receive all that the Creation has to offer. Now, reclench your fist. Ask about their personal experiences with "self-help." In 2008, Americans spent

132

over $11 billion dollars on self-help books, CDs, seminars and coaching—with a projected 6.2% annual growth through 2012.[399] The person most likely to buy a self-help book is someone who has already purchased a similar book within the past 18 months.[400] In other words, almost anyone who has tried to make themselves whole by "going it alone" has failed. "What are they getting for their money? In a word: hope."[401]

Now listen together to this cry of St. Paul: "Who will rescue me from this body of death?" (Romans 7:24). Speak the Scripture, "I do not understand my own actions. For I do not do what I want, but I do the very thing I hate" (Romans 7:15), and discuss why that might be. Reflect on their longing for hope in spite of their earthly suffering with Romans 5: 1-5:

> Therefore, since we are justified by faith, we have peace with God through our Lord Jesus Christ, through whom we have obtained access to this grace in which we stand; and we boast in our hope of sharing the glory of God. And not only that, but we also boast in our sufferings, knowing that suffering produces character, and character produces hope, and hope does not disappoint us, because God's love has been poured into our hearts through the Holy Spirit that has been given to us.

Those raised without any knowledge of the Christian faith will be surprised to learn that the same man wrote all three of these passages and that he was once the greatest "Jesus basher" of his day. In a remarkable reversal—the kind of thing Jesus implements routinely in the lives of the faithful—the man who had deep training in the realities of sin came to see the truth of the One who came to save us from it. Paul's story, we note, is not unlike that of St. Augustine, the church father who began to shape the concept of *homo incurvatus in se* by recognizing man's propensity to slump towards earthly delights and worries, willfully leaving God out of the picture. With his slick rhetoric, quick rise to the top of the Roman cultural elite, and well-documented lifestyle of "wine, woman and song," Augustine is a highly relatable figure for a modern day seeker in any American city. To hear his infamous words, "Grant me chastity and self-control, but please not yet,"[402] is to hear our own voice.

In the modern church's efforts to be "relevant," perhaps we would do well to spend less time trying to put Jesus in the neighborhood Starbucks, and instead, hold up as a mirror the tormented psyches of those who've struggled mightily with their faith; namely, from this thesis, Augustine and Luther. For all of Augustine's education, it was his personal observance that the body easily obeyed the mind—his knees bent, his lungs filled with air—but when *the mind commands itself* it "meets with resistance."[403] This led him closer to the heart of sin, but the process of faith was one of fits and starts:

'Let it be now,' I was saying to myself. 'Now is
the moment, let it be now,' and merely by saying
this I was moving toward the decision. I would
almost achieve it, but then fall just short; yet I did
not slip right down to my starting-point, but stood
aside to get my breath back. Then I would make a
fresh attempt, and now I was almost there, almost
there . . . I was touching the goal, grasping it . . .
and then I was not there, not touching, not
grasping it. I shrank from dying to death and
living to life, for ingrained evil was more
powerful in me than new-grafted good.[404]

This struggle of Augustine's was played out once again
by Luther, who came to see this push-pull as the very
reason the Church "had it wrong" when it came to this
notion of the new believer needing to "get it right." After
years of agonizing and soul-searching, Luther came to
understand that Man does not decide to believe, rather it
is a gift from God. Our refusal to yield "the decision" is
the last straw of our prideful and "turned in" state.
"Today if you hear his voice, do not harden your hearts"
(Hebrews 3: 7 & 15, and 4: 7b). To help a modern
secularist arrive at the moment where God might freely
give him that gift, we look briefly now at three of the
specific conditions reflective of *homo incurvatus in se*
cited in this thesis—anxiety, a disordered relationship to
technology, and apathy as non-participation—and how
they might be helpful in apologetic-style messaging.

using *homo incurvatus in se*
as an entry point for the
discussion of sin

why are we so anxious?

How can we use the fact of the rampant anxiety in modern America to begin a discussion of sin? We can first reassure a fretful listener that they are not alone; the cases of anxiety in the U.S. (as detailed in Chapter 2) have never been so high. We can explain that anxiety is part of a "family tree" which includes faith as well as anger. Anger is the *fight* response to threat, while anxiety is the *flight* response to threat.[405] "Anxiety and anger involve vigilance without faith and without love. They are untrusting, nonrelational responses to threat."[406] But the living God is a God of relationships. In every word of Scripture, and every act of every day, He is communicating with His people—or trying to. He does not want us to bear our worries alone: He wants us to lean on Him. We don't want to lean on Him—we don't even want to acknowledge Him—because we don't like feeling weak, and we don't want to give up control. But when we are living in constant anxiety, we are not in control; anxiety is. God helps reduce our anxiety—which is a disordered expression of the good, God-given gift of vigilance—by calling us into community with His people, who will help us shoulder the weight of our considerable worries.

> In Phillipians 4:3, Paul uses the word "yokefellow" (or "loyal friend"). "It refers to people who are united by a relational bond as close as family . . . a band of brothers. Sisters in the spirit. . . . Athletes together. . . Teammates. It's not 'take two verses and call me in the morning,' it's 'travel with a few safe spiritual friends morning, noon, and night . . . victory in anxiety comes in community.[407]

Pastor Kelleman shares some of the comments he hears regularly from his parishioners, thoughts that give voice to the experience of *homo incurvatus in se* made manifest in anxiety:

- "I'm constantly turned in upon myself and tuned in only to myself."
- "I'm consistently reflecting on myself and overly concerned with my life in a way that feels self-centered, obsessive, out of control, and abnormal."
- "I feel like something bad is going to happen that I can't control or handle—because I'm too weak."
- "I don't fight: I flee because I view the danger as bigger than my resources."
- I'm David against Goliath, but I don't see God in the scene."
- "Life is too hard for me. This situation is too big for me. I'm a child in an adult world."

Trusting that these are the words of those suffering from anxiety, we may approach with confidence when asking a nonbeliever to consider the possibility of God. "What if there were actually a God who created everything?" we might ask. "One who created you and has a plan for your life and is waiting patiently for you to just turn back in His direction so that he might be able to bless and help you?" We might suggest gently that sometimes the reason we feel so anxious and overwhelmed is that we were not designed to be "in charge" of everything. We were designed to live under the umbrella of the living God who "knit [us] together in [our] mother's womb[s]" (Psalm 139:13). Later, as these conversations evolve, and the root problem of choosing to "turn in" because we want to be our own God is faintly glimpsed, there is an opening for the idea of repentance—for owning whatever sin we can recognize, or are willing to admit—so that we might draw closer. And finally, as they began to understand sin as a condition they must live with—that we all must—they may be prepared for the full understanding of Christ Jesus as the name and face and Word of God through which we are to be reunited with, and healed by, Him.

why are we clinging to our devices?

As we saw in Chapter 2, this desire to focus on only what interests, amuses, inflates, or distracts us—to the exclusion of real human beings in our midst—is pure *homo incurvatus in se*. It is also a particular form of concupiscence that foments rapidly; the more we "turn in on" our self-created worlds, the more addicted we become to a life in our own little fiefdoms. This is one of the easiest forms of sinful behavior for a modern secularist to recognize: everyone knows they use their smart phones too much. New York comedian and journalist Dean Obeidaliah attempted what for many seems like the impossible: A Day Without a Cellphone.

> *At first, I felt liberated, like Neo in "The Matrix" when he took the red pill and could finally see the "real world." Instead of texting or checking my e-mail, I began to actually look at the people I was sharing the streets with. It truly resembled a movie set filled with extras from all walks of life ... It was truly exhilarating. For about 14 or 15 minutes or so. After that, I began to worry: What if someone needs to reach me? What if there is an important message waiting for me?. . . I soon began to feel phantom cell phone vibrations in the front left pocket of my jeans where my phone usually resides. My stress level started to escalate. I had to check my voice mail. But doing so would require me to engage in an activity I had not done for many years: Use a payphone. . . . While there's no short supply of pay phones in the Big Apple, there's apparently no one charged with cleaning them. The pay phones I saw looked and smelled like homeless people had confused them for bathrooms or had used them to clean certain*

parts of their anatomy. Despite the stench, I held my breath and made my call to retrieve my messages. How many did I have? Zero. . . . While relieved, my anxiety over my unchecked emails began to ratchet up . . . . I needed to find an Internet café. Sounds simple enough. But it's not. While establishments offering free Wi-Fi are everywhere, venues with computer terminals to use are not ... I began walking the streets asking people if they had seen an Internet café, like I was searching for my lost dog ... Fourteen blocks, two avenues and 45 minutes later, I finally observed a sign outside a slightly run-down deli that read, "Internet." And there I saw three computer terminals, whose best days were clearly behind them, available for rent at the reasonable rate of $2 for 12 minutes. So what e-mails had I missed? Nothing pressing, to be honest. They all could have waited until I returned home. As my cell phoneless day continued, I began to wonder: Would we actually talk to each other more if we weren't so attached to our gadgets? Would we be better people without our cell phones distracting us so often? Better spouses? Better sons or daughters? But I also realized that without my cell phone, I felt unconnected to my friends, my business, and the world. I began to feel lonely in the most crowded city in America ... My experiment without a cell phone taught me two valuable lessons. One, my cell phone is not just a

140

> *piece of technology; it is like Linus' security
> blanket in the "Peanuts" comic strip. Without it, I
> felt less comfortable. Less confident. I felt alone.[408]*

The Church has a tremendous opportunity to shine a light on this "disorder," and help guide people towards the awareness of this compulsive behavior as a manifestation of our Fallen natures. In the words of Romans 7:15: "We just can't help ourselves!" Even the culture recognizes this and is stepping up. In 2012, a popular L.A. restaurant called, ironically, Eva, began offering customers a 5% discount for ditching their phones at check in.[409] The chef estimates that 40-50% of their customers jump at the offer.[410] They are glad to have the excuse to "reconnect"[411] over a meal without distraction. How simple it would be for local churches to do the same—minus the discount. When we consider how hard it is for people to disconnect and be truly present, having a "cell phone check stand" in the narthex might be the greatest gift a 21st-century church could offer. From this simple, bold, countercultural step a conversation will naturally unfold about why we feel a need to be connected online 24/7. Why it seems so hard to quell the restlessness that technology stirs up. How filling up every empty moment with distractions leaves us little room to hear from God. Helping members, visitors, and the community let go of their "addiction" for a while, filling it instead with music, prayer, Scripture, the forgiving power of the Lord Jesus Christ, and some time with people far outside the scope of their given "friends" list, may be one of the easiest ways to demonstrate the move from *incurvatus in se* to *excurvatus ex se*. It will also begin to demonstrate the power of the Living, relational God, who comes to us face to face in other human beings so that we may know His love, grace, mercy, and forgiveness.

why have we stopped showing up?

As we saw in Chapter 3, there are many reasons for our downward slide in civic and communal participation: 1) we are too tired and anxious from trying to move up in the world, or trying to hold onto a spot in it; 2) we have no confidence in our own ability to make a difference; 3) unless a problem impacts our own immediate family, we don't see it as our concern; 4) we are afraid that if we do "one little thing" we'll get sucked into far more than we desire to give; 5) our identity is so individualistic that the idea of "joining" anything is anathema. So many people in America today are both lonely and bored, but offer them a chance to step outside, to lend a hand, to join in with some small effort, and they swat you away claiming to be "too busy." Czeslaw Milosz describes it this way:

> No one can call this failing simply laziness any longer; whatever it may once have been, nowadays it has returned to its original meaning: terror in the face of emptiness, apathy, depression. It's not isolated hermits, however, who are

experiencing its sting, but the masses in their millions.[412]

Milan Kundera also observes:

> I'd say that the quantity of boredom, if boredom is measureable, is much greater today than it was. Because the old occupations, at least most of them, were unthinkable without a passionate involvement: the peasants in love with their land . . . the shoemakers who knew every villager's feet by heart; the woodsmen; the gardeners . . . The meaning of life wasn't an issue, it was there with them, quite naturally, in their workshops, in their fields . . . Today we're all alike, all of us bound together by our shared apathy . . . [which] has become a passion. The one great collective passion of our time.[413]

One simple, excruciating outward turn and, according to C.S. Lewis, we would begin the journey into Life:

> For in self-giving, if anywhere, we touch a rhythm not only of all creation but of all being. . . . From the highest to the lowest, self exists to be abdicated and, by that abdication, becomes the more truly self, to be thereupon yet the more abdicated, and so forever.[414]

When we stand on the sidelines, disinterested, disinclined to bring our gifts to the table of Life, we fall deeper into our sinful, curved-in states. "The day is coming when you will wake to find, beyond all hope, that you have attained it [your God-given place in the world], or else, that it was within your reach and you have lost it forever."[415] These are the stakes. Presented in this way, the ears of the individualist may well be pricked up.

This tendency to disengage is a reflex of our *incurvatus* states. It affects the whole of the nation and each one of our communities. But it begins at home, with our loved ones, in our daily choices to turn away. The poet Scott Cairns captures the "first"[416] inward turn this way in his narrative poem *The Entrance of Sin*:

The Entrance of Sin

Yes, there was a tree, and upon it, among the wax leaves, an order of fruit which hung plentifully, glazed with dew of a given morning. And there had been some talk off and on—nothing specific—about forgoing the inclination to eat of it. But sin had very little to do with this or with any outright prohibition.

For sin had made its entrance long before the serpent spoke, long before the woman and the man had set their teeth to the pale, stringy flesh, which was, it turns out, also quite without flavor. Rather, sin had come in the midst of an evening stroll, when the woman had reached to take the man's hand and he withheld it.

In this way, the beginning of our trouble came to the garden almost without notice. And in later days, as the man and the woman wondered idly about their paradise, as they continued to enjoy the sensual pleasures of food and drink and spirited coupling, even as they sat marveling at the approach of evening and the more lush approach of sleep, they found within themselves a developing habit of resistance.

One supposed that, even then, this new taste for turning away might have been overcome, but that is assuming the two had found the result unpleasant. The beginning of loss was this: every time some manner of beauty was offered and declined, the subsequent isolation each conceived was irresistible. [417]

Each time we accept, rather than turn away from, the outstretched hand God enters in. Where "two or three are gathered in my name, I am there among them" (Matthew 18: 20), calling them into community through the Holy Spirit. Being a part of the "community of God"—even in the tiny gesture of receiving an outstretched hand—reduces anxiety, isolation, depression, apathy because it forms a relationship based on loving collaboration. Collaboration helps to tame the demon of competition, which so inflames our sense that we must spin our wheels harder and faster to keep up. In this way we are drawn further along the path that leads to Life. We cannot get there as long as we are turned in on ourselves, the sinful position of Pride.

> Unchastity, anger, greed, drunkenness, and all that, are mere fleabites in comparison: it was through Pride that the devil became the devil: Pride leads to every other vice: it is the complete anti-God state of mind. . . . Pride is *essentially* competitive—is competitive by its very nature—while the other vices are competitive only, so to speak, by accident. Pride gets no pleasure out of having something, only out of having more of it than the next man. We say that people are proud of being rich, or clever, or good-looking, but they are not. They are proud of being richer, or cleverer, of better-looking than others. If everyone else became equally rich, or clever or good-looking there would be nothing to be proud about ... Once the element of competition has gone, pride is gone.[418]

We will never be free of pride entirely, nor will be ever succeed in turning fully out to love and serve others—not in this lifetime, not until we are reunited with our Father in Heaven. Until then, C.S. Lewis offers us a glimpse of what it might look like when we can, at last, put down our guards, revel in the "unique vision"[419] of each soul, and frolic in the fields of the Lord like His children. Surely even those who have yet to yield to Him will recognize the beauty in this:

The first rule of the holy game . . . is that every player must by all means touch the ball and then immediately pass it on. To be found with it in your hands is a fault: to cling to it, death. But when it flies to and fro among the players too swift for eye to follow, and the great master Himself leads the revelry, giving Himself eternally to His creatures in the generation, and back to Himself in the sacrifice, of the Word, then indeed the eternal dance 'makes heaven drowsy with the harmony.' All pains and pleasures we have known on earth are early initiations in the movement of that dance.[420]

C.S. Lewis, *The Problem of Pain*

closing thoughts

The word "sin" is all but gone from 21st-century American culture. This presents an enormous challenge for the Church in communicating the priceless gifts of salvation and forgiveness. Since the Gospel has no meaning without the promises of the atonement, those who dedicate themselves to the Great Commission must find new ways to make sin understood. The image of *homo incurvatus in se* can help by 1) demonstrating that sin is a state not an act, 2) giving a visual reference for how it looks when we cling to our own wills and effectively block out the only real help there is, 3) creating an opportunity for dialogue about the paradigm of Life as envisioned by the Creator, 4) connecting the dots from "sin" to the many forms of common suffering and brokenness we see in our culture today, 5) reclaiming the voice of the sincere Christian spirit by reintroducing the teachings, struggles, and joys of Paul, Augustine, and Luther, 6) countering our individualistic society with the promise of the "outward-turned" life of collaborative community in the Body of Christ.

This is the endgame. May the work of these pages prove of some value in helping those outside His love to recognize their *curvatus* nature and, in response, turn back to the Lord "with all their hearts, soul, and mind."

about the author

Heather Choate Davis began her writing career as an advertising copywriter. Over the past 30 years, she's written screenplays, teleplays, one-acts, liturgies, and books: *Baptism by Fire*, *The Pitcher's Mom*, and *Elijah & the SAT: Reflections on a Hairy, Old, Desert Prophet and the Benchmarking of our Children's Lives*. She has taught creative writing and Junior Great Books, created an original, arts-based vespers called The Renaissance Service™, and led retreats at a high desert monastery. After receiving her MA in Theology from Concordia University, Irvine, she co-founded a company called icktank. Icktank's mission is to reclaim the Christian conversation by demystifying insider language; its first release is the co-authored book *Loaded Words: Freeing 12 Hard Bible Words from Their Baggage*. This book, *Man Turned in on Himself,* is a mainstream release of Davis's MA thesis, which was written to go out into the world and be of some use.

Davis is an L.A. native. She lives with her husband Lon in Mar Vista, CA where they practice loving their neighbor on a "commune-esque" cul-de-sac. You can find out more about her work at heatherchoatedavis.com or at icktank.com.

endnotes

[1] From the Greek, *hamartia*, an archer's term which is used throughout scripture to describe "sin."

[2] John Portmann, *The History of Sin: Its Evolution to Today and Beyond* (Lanham, Rowman & Littlefield Publishers, 2007),xiii-xiv.

[3] Ibid.

[4] Ibid., xvi.

[5] Ibid., 59.

[6] St. Augustine, *The City of God* (New York, Penguin Books, 1984), 569.

[7] Pastor Tim Kelleher quoted by Cathy Lynn Grossman, "Has the notion of Sin been Lost," USA Today (April 16, 2008) http://www.usatoday.com/news/religion/2008-03-19-sin_N.htm?loc=interstitialskip (Accessed October 20, 2011)

[8] Portmann, xiii-xiv.

[9] St. Augustine, *The City of God* (New York, Modern Library, 1993), 445.

[10] St. Augustine, *Exposition on the Book of Psalms*, ed. Philip Schaff (New York, Christian Literature Publishing Company, 1886), accessed from http://www.ccel.org/ccel/schaff/npnf108.txt, May 12, 2012.

[11] Augustine, *Exp on the Psalms*.

[12] Ibid.

[13] Ibid.

[14] Ibid.

[15] The final line adds "Yet the 'seat of pestilence' may be more appropriately understood of hurtful doctrine; 'whose word spreadeth like a canker.'" Interesting to note that this revered church father uses the term "hurtful doctrine" as opposed to the more popular "false doctrine." It would seem to reveal a heart for souls often not seen in the embattled language of the Councils.

[16] St. Augustine, *Exposition on the Book of Psalms*,1.

[17] St. Augustine, *The Works of Saint Augustine: A Translation for the 21st Century, Sermons II (20-50) of the Old Testament*, trans. Edmund Hill, O.P., ed. John E. Rotelle, O.S.A. (Brooklyn, New City Press, 1990) 31.

[18] International Standard Bible Encyclopedia Online, s.v. "Concupiscence," http://www.internationalstandardbible.com/C/concupiscence.h

152

tml (accessed September 24, 2012).

[19] Anders Nygren, *Agape and Eros* (Philadelphia, Westminster Press, 1953), 485.

[20] Matt Jenson, *The Gravity of Sin* (London, T & T Clark, 2006), 24.

[21]Nygren, citing Augustine's Commentary on Psalm 122, 483.

[22] Ibid., 485.

[23] Jenson,21.

[24] St Augustine, *The City of God* (Penguin Books), 547.

[25] Jenson, 7.

[26] Ibid.

[27] St. Augustine, *The City of God* (Modern), 386.

[28] St. Augustine, *The Works of Saint Augustine: A Translation for the 21st Century, Sermons II (20-50) of the Old Testament*, trans. Edmund Hill, O.P., ed. John E. Rotelle, O.S.A. (Brooklyn, New City Press, 1990) 30.

[29] Ibid.

[30] St .Augustine (Sermons 20-50), 30.

[31] St. Augustine, *The City of God* (Modern), 388.

[32] Ibid., 460.

[33] Jenson,26.

[34] Jenson,21.

[35] Ibid.

[36] Jenson, 32.

[37] Ibid., 11.

[38] St. Augustine, *Exposition on the Book of Psalms*, 1.

[39] Jenson, 47, citing *Luther's Progress* (London, SMC Press, 1951), 40.

[40] Ibid., 47.

[41] Ibid., 60.

[42] Martin Luther, "Lectures on Romans: Glosses and Scholia," Hilton C. Oswald, vol. 25 of *Luther's Works* (St. Louis, Concordia Publishing House, 1972), 385.

[43] Nygren, 483.

[44] Ibid., 485-86, footnotes.

[45] Jenson, 47.

[46] Jenson, 64, with reference to LW 25: 222.

[47] Ibid., 65, including text from LW 25: 418-19.

[48] Jenson, 73, referencing McCue, "*Simul justus et peccator* in Augustine, Aquina, and Luther," p. 90.

[49] LW 25:276.

[50] LW 25:345.

[51] LW 25:345.

[52] NETBible.org, Genesis 2, http://bible.org/netbible/, accessed July 20, 2012.

[53] Ibid.

[54] Jenson, 16.

[55] Portmann, 9.

[56] Jenson, 16, referencing Richard Chenevix Trench, *Exposition of the Sermon on the Mount* (London: Macmillan and Co., 3rd ed, 1869), 116.

[57] Marie Vejrup Nielsen, *Sin and Selfish Genes: Christian and Biological Narratives* (Leuven, Petters, 2010), 11.

[58] Jenson, 69 referencing Regin Prenter, *Spiritus Creator* (trans. John M. Jensen; Philidelphia: Muhlenberg Press, 1953), 225.

[59] LW 25:366 This idea of becoming pliable and willing is implied rather than expressed. What *is* expressed here is man's wanting to *be* the potter, and, when realizing that is not possible, fleeing the Spirit of God.

[60] Jenson, 76.

[61] LW 25:475.

[62] Ibid.

[63] Jenson, 90.

[64] Ibid., 71.

[65] LW 25:262-3.

[66] LW 25:475.

[67] Jenson, 89.

[68] Ibid., 92 including reference to LW 25:447.

[69] LW 25:16, 197-98.

[70] LW 25:448.

[71] Although he cites this in the extreme, I believe that his sense of vocation and call would support the idea that *some* were, in fact, called to lead lives set apart fully for God and prayer.

[72] Jenson, 92.

[73] Ibid.

[74] John Winthrop quoted in David G. Myers, *The American Paradox: Spiritual Hunger in an Age of Plenty* (New Haven, Yale University Press, 2000), 194.

[75] Claude H. Van Tine, *The Causes of the War of Independence* (New York, Houghton Miflin, 1922), 318.

[76] John Winthrop, "A Model of Christian Charity," written aboard

the Arbella, 1630.

[77] David G. Myers, *The American Paradox: Spiritual Hunger in an Age of Plenty* (New Haven, Yale University Press, 2000), 162.

[78] Alexis de Tocqueville: *Democracy in America*, ed. J.P. Mayer (New York: Knopf, 1991), pp. 506-8, quoted in Myers' *The American Paradox*, p. 162.

[79] William E. Hudson, *American Democracy in Peril: Seven Challenges to America's Future* (Chatham, N.Y.; Chatham House, 1995), 72.

[80] Tocqueville, 692.

[81] Ibid., 506.

[82] Myers, 163.

[83] Ibid.

[84] Robert N. Bellah, Richard Madsen, William M. Sullivan, Ann Swidler, and Steven M. Tipton: *Habits of the Heart: Individualism and Commitment in American Life* (Berkeley, CA: University of California Press, 1985), 6.

[85] Time: Business & Money "Millions of Pet Halloween Costumes? Why we Spend More and More on Pets,"http://business.time.com/2012/10/04/millions-on-pet-halloween-costumes-why-we-spend-more-and-more-on-pets/?iid=pf-main-lede/ (accessed Oct. 07, 2012).

[86] Reuters, "Fat and Getting Fatter: U.S. Obesity rates to soar by 2030," http://www.reuters.com/article/2012/09/18/us-obesity-us-idUSBRE88H0RA20120918 (accessed Nov. 21, 2012).

[87] CNN online, "Going to Extremes: Eating Disorders," http://www.cnn.com/interactive/2012/03/health/infographic.eating.disorders/index.html (accessed Nov. 21, 2012).

[88] Myers, 176.

[89] Portmann, xvi.

[90] Ibid., xvii.

[91] Charles Murray, *Coming Apart: The State of White America, 1960-2010*, (New York, Crown Forum, 2012), 291.

[92] Myers, 165, quoting the rationale Woody Allen gave to explain his affair with his adopted daughter.

[93] Meyers, 165.

[94] Ibid.

[95] Ibid.

[96] PBS Online, "The Pill: Timeline," http://www.pbs.org/wgbh/amex/pill/timeline/timeline2.html

(accessed Nov. 21, 2012).

[97] Fritz Perls, "Gestalt Therapy Prayer", 1969.

[98] Myers, 163.

[99] Bobby McFerrin, 1988, from the album "Simple Pleasures." The quote is taken from the Indian mystic, Meher Baba, whose full expression included both personal responsibility and a divine master—"Do your best. Then, don't worry; be happy in My love. I will help you."
http://en.wikipedia.org/wiki/Don%27t_Worry,_Be_Happy (accessed Feb. 20, 2013).

[100] Galatians 6: 7, paraphrase.

[101] Portmann, 105.

[102] ParentsTV, http://www.parentstv.org/PTC/facts/mediafacts.asp (accessed Nov. 26, 2012).

[103] Pew Research Center, "The Generation Gap and the 2012 Election," http://www.people-press.org/2011/11/03/section-8-domestic-and-foreign-policy-views/ (accessed Nov. 24, 2012).

[104] Murray, 160. He refers to 1930 book, *Sex, Culture, and Myth* by Bronislaw Malinowski, which concluded that "the principle of legitimacy" amounted to a "universal cultural norm." *Every* culture, he concluded had a norm that "no child should be brought into the world without a man—and one man at that—assuming the role of sociological father, that is, guardian and protector, the male link between the child and the rest of the community."

[105] Contemporary social media poster, source unknown.

[106] C.S. Lewis, *The Problem of Pain*, (New York, Harper One, 1940), 48.

[107] Lewis, 49.

[108] Lewis., 48.

[109] Ibid., 59.

[110] Ibid., 71.

[111] American Psychiatric Association (2000). *Diagnostic and Statistical Manual of Mental Disorders* (4th Ed., Text Revision). Washington DC: American Psychiatric Association.

[112] Merriam-Webster Online: Anxiety

[113] Patrick Gardiner, *Nineteenth Century Philosophy*, (New York, The Free Press, 1969).

[114] Arne Gron, *The Concept of Anxiety* in Soren Kierkegaard, (Macon, Mercer University Press, 2008), 19, citing Soren Kierkegaard, *The Concept of Anxiety*, 152.

[115] Robert W. Kellemen, *Anxiety: Anatomy and Cure* (Phillipsburg, P & R Publishing, 2012), 10.

[116] Sharon Begley, "In the Age of Anxiety, are we all Mentally Ill?" Reuters.com, July 13, 2012, http://www.reuters.com/article/2012/07/13/us-usa-health-anxiety-idUSBRE86C07820120713 (accessed November 26, 2012).

[117] Ibid.

[118] American Accreditation Healthcare Commission: Anxiety, as reviewed in the *New York Times*: Health Guide, Review Date: 2/8/2012, Harvey Simon, MD, Editor-in-Chief, Associate Professor of Medicine, Harvard Medical School; Physician, Massachusetts General Hospital. Also reviewed by David Zieve, MD, MHA, Medical Director, A.D.A.M., Inc. http://health.nytimes.com/health/guides/disease/generalized-anxiety-disorder/risk-factors.html (accessed November 26, 2012).

[119] Ibid.

[120] Peter Gray, "The Dramatic Rise of Anxiety and Depression in Children and Adolescents: Is It Connected to the Decline in Play and Rise in Schooling?" *Psychology Today*, January 5, 2012 http://www.psychologytoday.com/blog/freedom-learn/201001/the-dramatic-rise-anxiety-and-depression-in-children-and-adolescents-is-it (accessed November 26, 2012).

[121] Gray, *Psychology Today.*

[122] Ibid.

[123] Gray, *Psychology Today.*

[124] Ibid.

[125] Jean M. Twenge, *Generation Me: Why Today's Young Americans are more Confident, Assertive, Entitled—and more Miserable than ever Before* (New York, Free Press, 2007), cover.

[126] Gray, *Psychology Today.*

[127] Ibid.

[128] Ruth Whippman, "America the Anxious," *New York Times*, Opinionator: Anxiety, September 22, 2012 http://opinionator.blogs.nytimes.com/2012/09/22/america-the-anxious/#more-134293 (Accessed November 17, 2012).

[129] Myers, 165.

[130] Sarah D. Sparks, "Tests Reveal Varied Facets of U.S. Students' Competitiveness," Education Week, August 18, 2011, http://blogs.edweek.org/edweek/inside-school-research/2011/08/back_to_school_means_back.html (accessed November 27, 2012).

[131] Whippman.

[132] Gron,113.

[133] Barna Group, "Self-Described Christians Dominate America but Wrestle with Four Areas of Spiritual Depth," September 13, 2011, http://www.barna.org/faith-spirituality/524-self-described-christians-dominate-america-but-wrestle-with-four-aspects-of-spiritual-depth (accessed November 29, 2012).

[134] Kellemen, 7.

[135] Ibid.

[136] Ibid.

[137] Ibid., 8.

[138] Ibid., 16.

[139] Marc Galanter, M.D., *Spirituality and the Healthy Mind: Science, Therapy, and the need for Personal Meaning*, (New York, Oxford University Press, 2005), 88, citing Christopher Lasch, *The Culture of Narcissism*.

[140] Begley, Reuters.

[141] Dan G. Blazer, *The Age of Melancholy: "Major Depression" and its Social Origins* (New York, Routledge, 2005), 15.

[142] Andrew Solomon, *The Noonday Demon: An Atlas of Depression*, (New York, Scribner, 2011), 65.

[143] Solomon, 65.

[144] World Health Organization, Media Centre: Depression, October 2012, http://www.who.int/mediacentre/factsheets/fs369/en/ (accessed November 30, 2012)

[145] Blazer, 3.

[146] Solomon, 25.

[147] Portmann, 130.

[148] Ibid.

[149] Solomon, 294.

[150] Kathleen Norris, *Acedia & Me: A Marriage, Monks and a Writer's Life*, (New York, Riverhead Books, 2008),76.

[151] Blazer, 6.

[152] Ibid., 3. "70% of those who take antidepressant drugs respond."
[153] Blazer, 6.
[154] Ibid., 7
[155] Ibid.
[156] Ibid.
[157] Ibid., 11.
[158] Ibid., 40.
[159] Ibid., 53, summarizing Michael Norden, *Beyond Prozac*.
[160] Ibid., 54.
[161] Ibid, 12.
[162] Ibid., 43.
[163] Ibid.
[164] Ibid., 44.
[165] Ibid.
[166] Norris, 3.
[167] Ibid., 21.
[168] Ibid.
[169] Ibid., 45-46.
[170] John N. Blackwell, *The Noonday Demon: Recognizing and Conquering the Deadly Sin of Sloth*, (New York, The Crossroad Publishing Company, 2004), 26.
[171] Blazer, 17.
[172] Blackwell, 12.
[173] Sting (Gordon Sumner) & the Police, "O My God" from the album *Synchronicity*, 1983.
[174] Solomon, 15.
[175] Mark Brown, Global Scope Media, Daily Inspiration, https://www.facebook.com/MarkBrown.page?ref=ts&fref=ts
[176] Tim Farrington, *A Hell of Mercy: A Meditation on Depression and the Dark Night of the Soul*, (New York, Harper One, 2009), 69.
[177] New Advent Catholic Encyclopedia, St. John of the Cross http://www.newadvent.org/cathen/08480a.htm (Accessed December 3, 2012).
[178] Solomon, 15.
[179] Blackwell, 12.
[180] Robert D. Putnam, *Bowling Alone: The Collapse and Revival of American Community*, (New York, Simon & Schuster, 2000), 217.
[181] Ibid., 239.
[182] Ibid., 217.

[183] BLS American Time Use Survey, A.C. Nielsen Co., Television Watching Statistics, February 7th, 2012, http://www.statisticbrain.com/television-watching-statistics/ (accessed December 22, 2014).

[184] Putnam, 240. Citing British researchers Sue Bowden and Avner Offer.

[185] Ibid., 242. Summarizing theories of Joshua Meyrowitz and Roderick Hart.

[186] Putnam, 235.

[187] Ibid., 223.

[188] Pew Internet & American Life Forum: Social Networking, November 13, 2012 http://pewinternet.org/Commentary/2012/March/Pew-Internet-Social-Networking-full-detail.aspx (accessed December 3, 2012).

[189] Pew Internet, "Social Isolation and New Technology," November 4, 2009. http://www.pewinternet.org/Reports/2009/18--Social-Isolation-and-New-Technology.aspx (accessed December 3 , 2012).

[190] Ibid.

[191] Sherry Turkle, *Alone Together: Why We expect more from Technology and Less from Each Other* (New York, Basic Books, 2011), xi.

[192] Stephanie Miot, "Social Media use Exploded in 2012, Led by Pinterest," *PC Magazine*, December 3, 2012, http://www.pcmag.com/article2/0,2817,2412785,00.asp?kc=PCRSS03069TX1K0001121 (accessed December 4, 2012)

[193] Ibid.

[194] Mike Snider, "Even When You Gotta Go, Social Media Goes Too," *USA Today*, December 3, 2012, http://www.usatoday.com/story/tech/2012/12/02/social-media-use-rises/1738009/ (accessed December 4, 2012).

[195] Turkle, xii.

[196] Jodi L. Whitaker & Brad J. Bushman "Online Dangers: Keeping Children and Adolescents Safe," *Washington & Lee Law Review*, 66 (2009), 1058.

[197] Sharon H. Thompson & Eric Lougheed, "Frazzled by Facebook? An Exploratory Study of Gender Differences in Social Network Communication Among Undergraduate Men and

Women," *College Student Journal*, March 2012, Vol. 1., 96.

[198] Ibid.

[199] Ibid.

[200] Ibid.

[201] Augustine, *City of God*, (Modern, 32)

[202] Turkle, 11.

[203] Ibid., 12.

[204] Ibid.

[205] Ibid, 10.

[206] Ibid.

[207] Turkle, 10,11.

[208] Ibid., 23.

[209] Ibid., 10.

[210] Ibid., 24

[211] Ibid., 9

[212] Ibid.

[213] Norris, 114.

[214] Portmann, 6.

[215] Turkle, 50.

[216] Turkle., 50.

[217] Ibid., 28.

[218] Ibid, 52.

[219] Ibid. 51.

[220] Ibid.

[221] Myers, 269.

[222] Ibid.

[223] Garrett Hardin, "The Tragedy of the Commons," *Science*, December 13, 1968, Vol 162, 1244.

[224] Hardin

[225] Portmann, xvi.

[226] David B. Capes, Rodney Reeves and E. Randolph Richards, *Rediscovering Paul: An Introduction to His World, Letters and Theology* (Downers Grove, IL, InterVarsity Press, 2007), 24.

[227] Capes, 24.

[228] Plato, Gorgias, Excerpt 1, translated by Benjamin Jowett (Project Guttenberg eBook, 2008), 14.

[229] Portmann, xiv.

[230] Mick Jagger & Keith Richards, "I'm Free," from the album *Out of our Heads* (1965)

[231] Portmann, xiv.

[232] Murray, 12.

[233] Myers, 8.

[234] Ezra Klein, "Twelve Facts about Guns and Mass Shootings in the United States," *The Washington Post*, December 14, 2012. http://www.washingtonpost.com/blogs/wonkblog/wp/2012/12/14/nine-facts-about-guns-and-mass-shootings-in-the-united-states/ (accessed December 20, 2012).

[235] Gary J. Gates, "How Many are Lesbian, Gay, Bisexual, and Transgender?" The Williams Institute, April 2011, http://williamsinstitute.law.ucla.edu/wp-content/uploads/Gates-How-Many-People-LGBT-Apr-2011.pdf (accessed December 26. 2012).

[236] Ibid.

[237] Ibid.

[238] Myers, 36 citing Helen E. Fisher, "After All, Maybe it's Biology," *Psychology Today*, March/April, 1993, 40-45.

[239] Haeberle; it is important to note that most marriages in ancient Greece (as well as in Rome) were arranged. The institution was taken very seriously, but it was understood that men would seek outlets for any additional sexual needs outside the marriage—in Greece, through concubines, and in Rome, with mistresses or other men.

[240] Haeberle, 1.

[241] Myers, 38.

[242] Myers, 36, summarizing the thinking of anthropologist Bronislaw Malinowski from *Sex, Culture, and Myth*, 1930.

[243] Myers, 38.

[244] St Augustine, *The City of God* (Penguin Books), 547.

[245] D'vera Cohn, Jeffrey Passel, Wendy Wang, Gretchen Livingston, "Barely Half of U.S. Adults are Married—A record Low." Pew Research Center, December 14, 2011. http://www.pewsocialtrends.org/2011/12/14/barely-half-of-u-s-adults-are-married-a-record-low/?src=sdt-carousel (accessed December 26, 2012)

[246] Pew Social Trends, "The Decline of Marriage and Rise of New Families," November 18, 2010. http://www.pewsocialtrends.org/2010/11/18/the-decline-of-marriage-and-rise-of-new-families/2/#ii-overview (accessed December 26, 2012)

[247] Myers, 40, citing retired Princeton University family historian,

Lawrence Stone, "The Road to Polygamy," *New York Review*, March 2, 1989.

[248] Murray, 129.

[249] Ibid., 134.

[250] Murray, 135.

[251] Ibid, 130.

[252] As this thesis endeavors to make sin recognizable to a nonbeliever, there will be no "proof points" on religiosity, a message that tends to fall on deaf ears and reinforce a "priggish" view of the Church. Rather, the focus throughout, and particularly in the conclusion, will be on the language and ideas that might help people draw closer to the Gospel message.

[253] Murray.

[254] Ibid., 128.

[255] Ibid., 129.

[256] Myers, 15.

[257] Leon R. Kass, "Man and Woman: An Old Story" *First Things*, November 1991 http://www.firstthings.com/article/2007/12/002-man-and-woman-an-old-story-29 (accessed July 17, 2012).

[258] Murray, 137.

[259] Ibid., 136.

[260] Ibid.

[261] Ibid.

[262] Ibid., 134.

[263] Ibid., 15.

[264] Ibid.

[265] Ibid..

[266] Myers, 14.

[267] Ibid., 18.

[268] LW 25:299.

[269] Myers, 30.

[270] Murray, 157.

[271] Myers, 55.

[272] Ibid., 29.

[273] Ibid.

[274] Meyers, 30.

[275] St. Augustine, *The Confessions*, Translated by Maria Boulding O.S.B. (New York, Vintage Spiritual Classics, 1997), 37.

[276] St. Augustine, *The Confessions*, 55.

[277] Myers, 14.
[278] Portmann, 4.
[279] Audrey Barrick, "Christian Divorce Rate Identical to National Average," *The Christian Post*, April 4, 2008. http://www.christianpost.com/news/study-christian-divorce-rate-identical-to-national-average-31815/ (accessed December 29, 2012).
[280] Murray, 289.
[281] Ibid..
[282] Ibid., 162.
[283] Murray, 290.
[284] Ibid.
[285] Jenson, 73. Includes concepts gleaned from McCue, "Simul iustus et peccator in Augustine, Aquinas, and Luther," 90; and Steinmetz, Luther and Staupitz, 106.
[286] Murray, 134.
[287] Guttmacher Institute, "Contraceptive Use in the United States," http://www.guttmacher.org/pubs/fb_contr_use.html (accessed December 29, 2012).
[288] Jose Martinez, On Central, November 21, 2012, citing the November 23 edition, Mortality and Morbidity Report (CDC) http://www.oncentral.org/news/2012/11/21/cdc-18-percent-us-pregnancies-end-abortion/ (accessed December 29, 2012).
[289] Ibid.
[290] Murray, 159.
[291] Ibid.,12.
[292] Ibid,145.
[293] Ibid., 149.
[294] Ibid., 158.
[295] Ibid, 160.
[296] Ibid., 161.
[297] Ibid., 160.
[298] Ibid.
[299] Ibid.
[300] Ibid., 162.
[301] Ibid.
[302] Ibid., 3.
[303] Ibid., 167.
[304] Ibid., 164-5.
[305] Myers, 31.

[306] Ibid.

[307] Pew Social Trends, "The Decline of Marriage and Rise of New Families."

[308] Ibid.

[309] Doyle McManus, "The Upward Mobility Gap," *L.A. Times,* January 2, 2011, http://articles.latimes.com/2011/jan/02/opinion/la-oe-mcmanus-twous-20110102 (accessed July 27, 2012).

[310] McManus.

[311] Norris, 135.

[312] Murray, 288.

[313] Ibid.

[314] Ibid., 288-9.

[315] Murray, 179.

[316] Ibid., 181.

[317] Joe Klein, "Where Checks Alone Can't Help," *Time*, June 25, 2012, 32, quoting an unemployed former addict in the Appalachian town of Gallipolis, Ohio.

[318] Murray, 181.

[319] Myers, 44.

[320] Murray, 181.

[321] Ibid., 182.

[322] Ibid., 227.

[323] LW 25:345.

[324] Gustav Wingren, *Luther on Vocation*, translated by Carl C. Rasmussen (Evansville, Ballast Press, 1999), 1.

[325] Ibid.

[326] Ibid.

[327] Wingren, 1.

[328] Gene Edward Veith, Jr., *God at Work: Your Christian Vocation in All of Life* (Wheaton, Crossway Book, 2002), 14.

[329] Wingren, 8.

[330] Vieth, 41.

[331] Murray, 247.

[332] Ibid.

[333] Veith, 49.

[334] Anand Giridharadas, "Keeping One's Work in Perspective," New York Times, December 28, 2012. http://www.nytimes.com/2012/12/29/us/29iht-currents29.html?smid=fb-share&_r=0 (accessed December 29,

2012).

[335] Jenson, 7.

[336] Murray, 100.

[337] Ibid., citing Tocqueville, 1840, vol. 2, Google Books.

[338] Ibid., 26.

[339] Ibid., 50.

[340] Ibid.

[341] Murray, 61.

[342] Ibid.

[343] Ibid., 59.

[344] Ibid., 52.

[345] Ibid., 57.

[346] Murray, 69.

[347] Ibid., 78.

[348] Ibid., 84.

[349] Ibid., 54.

[350] Ibid.

[351] Nicholas Lehman, *The Big Test: The Secret History of the American Meritocracy* (New York, Ferrar, Strauss, and Giroux, 2000), 110.

[352] Ibid., 185.

[353] Murray, 101.

[354] Ibid.

[355] Luther, "Lectures on Romans: Glosses and Scholia," 385.

[356] Andres Duany, Elizabeth Plater-Zyberk and Jeff Speck, *Suburban Nation: The Rise of Sprawl and the Decline of the American Dream*, (New York, North Point Press, 2000), 45.

[357] Duany, 40.

[358] Duany., 43.

[359] Ibid., 44.

[360] Duany, 4.

[361] Ibid., 6-7.

[362] Ibid., 25.

[363] Ibid.

[364] Duany, 45.

[365] Murray, 12.

[366] Ibid., 238.

[367] Ibid., 241. Compared to the participation level in 1963.

[368] Putnam, 252.

[369] Ibid., 1.
[370] Ibid., 1.
[371] Murray, 239.
[372] Ibid.
[373] Ibid.
[374] Ibid., 240.
[375] Putnam, 253
[376] YPulse, "Five facts about the Millennial Vote and the 2012 Election," November 5, 2012, http://www.ypulse.com/post/view/5-facts-about-the-millennial-vote-and-the-2012-election, (accessed January 1, 2012).
[377] YPulse.
[378] Putnam, 257.
[379] Ibid., 258, citing political biographer Michael Delli Carpini.
[380] Murray, 242.
[381] Ibid., 246.
[382] Ibid., 267.
[383] Ibid.
[384] Putnam, 334.
[385] Ibid.
[386] Martin E. P. Seligman, "Boomer Blues," *Psychology Today*, October 1988, 50-55, quoted in Putnam, 335.
[387] Mark R. McMinn, *Psychology, Theology and Spirituality in Christian Counseling*, (Carol Stream, Tyndale House, 1996), 41.
[388] Anne Herbert quoted in Carl Skrade, "The Opposite of Sin is Love," *Society and Original Sin: Ecumenical Essays on the Impact of the Fall (New York, Paragon House, 1985).*
[389] Lewis, 70 & 71.
[390] Mike Middendorf, "Preaching and Teaching: Exegetical Reflections," 1.
[391] Ibid., citing Alan Richardson, *A Theological Wordbook of the Bible* (New York: Macmillan, 1950), 171-72. This is based upon the work of C.H.Dodd, The Apostolic Preaching and Its Developments (New York: Harper, 1937).
[392] Lewis, 48.
[393] Myers, 257.
[394] Ibid.
[395] Ibid., 258.
[396] Ibid., 259.

[397] Myers, 258.

[398] Portmann, xi.

[399] Melanie Linder, "What People are Still Willing to Pay For," *Forbes*, January 15, 2009, http://www.forbes.com/2009/01/15/self-help-industry-ent-sales-cx_ml_0115selfhelp.html (accessed February, 23, 2013).

[400] Ibid.

[401] Ibid.

[402] St. Augustine, *The Confessions*, 159.

[403] St. Augustine (Vintage), 162.

[404] St. Augustine (Vintage), 165.

[405] Kelleman, 9.

[406] Ibid., 10.

[407] Kelleman, 21.

[408] Dean Obeideliah, "A Day Without a Cell Phone," CNN, September 26, 2012, http://www.cnn.com/2012/09/26/opinion/obeidallah-cell-phone (accessed February 13, 2013).

[409] Erin Kim, "Restaurant offers a 5% Discount to Eat Without your Phone," CNN Money, August 16, 2012, http://money.cnn.com/2012/08/16/technology/restaurant-cell-phone-discount/index.html (accessed February 27, 2013).

[410] Kim, CNN Money.

[411] Ibid.

[412] Norris, 312, citing Czeslaw Milosz, *The Garden of Knowledge*,

[413] Ibid., 318, citing Milan Kundera, *Identity.*

[414] Lewis, 157.

[415] Ibid., 152.

[416] This is obviously not intended to be read as doctrine, but as a creative way of allowing the truth of *homo incurvatus in se* to be recognized.

[417] Scott Cairns, *Recovered Body*, (Wichita, Eighth Day Press, 2003), 52.

[418] C.S. Lewis, *Mere Christianity* (New York, Harper One, 1952), 122.

[419] Lewis, *The Problem of Pain*, 155.

[420] Ibid., 158.

Made in the USA
Charleston, SC
18 January 2016